GW01161699

LaGrange Craigavon

LaGrange

William McCarroll   Robert Curran   Clark Johnson

Cottage Publications

First published by Cottage Publications,
Donaghadee, N. Ireland 1999.
Copyrights Reserved.
© Craigavon SCI Committee / LIFE
All rights reserved.
No part of this book may be reproduced or
stored on any media without the express
written permission of the publishers.
Design & origination in Northern Ireland.
Printed & bound in Singapore.

ISBN 1 900935 14 7

Preamble

This publication seeks to celebrate and highlight the significance of the relationship which has been developing between LaGrange, Georgia, USA and Craigavon, Northern Ireland, since contact was first made in 1993. The formalisation of the linkage in 1996 through Sister City International became the catalyst for a programme of civic, cultural, sport, business and education exchanges.

The photographs and paintings reflect the perceptions of the photographers and artists, from the communities involved, following visits to their respective Sister Cities ie; The Artist and Author from Craigavon have provided almost all the images of LaGrange and vice-versa. It is by no means an exhaustive authority on the history of the areas involved nor does it claim to have captured all the facets of life that exists in them. It is hoped, however, that through the images and text, the appetite of the reader will be whet to the extent that they will wish to visit their Sister City. If it further inspires them to get involved with the work of the LaGrange International Friendship Exchange (LIFE) Committee or the Craigavon Sister City International Committee to extend the benefits of the relationship to a greater number of citizens then so much the better.

Acknowledgments

"THANK YOU" is a small phrase but it comes with deep gratitude and much affection to EVERYONE who contributed time, effort, talent, brain, and brawn in helping to make this publication come to fruition. With grateful thanks to Clark Johnson, Troup County Historian, who was BORN! knowing the history of LaGrange, Troup County, and Georgia! and who so willingly and cheerfully shared that wealth of knowledge; to the handsome John Lawrence and lovable Alexander Kalinin for sharing their talent and expertise. With many thanks to the City of LaGrange, Mayor, and Council, especially dependable friend, Joe Maltese, and the Callaway Foundation, Inc. for their continued funding and support of LIFE; to the LaGrange/Troup Cty. Chamber of Commerce, LaGrange Fire Dept., LaGrange College, Callaway Gardens, and the people that gave freely of their time and properties. AND! lastly-with much love, gratitude, and appreciation to the best husband in the world, Dick Ross, who has given so freely of his money, office, home, and wife to LIFE.

Margaret Ross

The Photographer

Born in 1958, Robert Curran spent the early part of his life living on a farm in the beautiful County of Armagh. The surrounding countryside inspiring him to a love of photography.

He left school in 1976 to begin a career in sales, again travelling through the beautiful countryside of N. Ireland. It fuelled an inner desire to become a professional photographer, something he already enjoyed doing in his spare time.

Twelve years ago he took up the challenge and set up his own business in Photography and Graphic Design allowing him to design brochures and organise exhibitions for N. Ireland Companies.

In Robert's own words "To be given the opportunity to contribute to this book was an honour beyond words. The beautiful countryside and wonderful people of LaGrange has left a memory in my life that will never be forgotten".

The Author

Forrest Clark Johnson, III – a ninth generation native of Troup County, graduate of the University of Georgia with a Masters in History, has served as a History Teacher in Troup County since 1974 and County Historian since 1990. He has authored eleven books on local history and genealogy and works with the Troup County Archives, part time.

The Artist

A member of the Rotary Club, First Methodist Church and Sons of the American Revolution, he also serves on the Board of the LaGrange Symphony. He and his wife, Deborah have two sons and a daughter.

painting as a career, and has served as Secretary of the Ulster Watercolour Society. He currently teaches leisure watercolour classes in Craigavon.

An artist in traditional style, he exhibits in Switzerland, Scotland and throughout N. Ireland.

A native of Lurgan, William McCarroll spent the early part of his career as a textile designer and illustrator in the local linen industry. With the decline in linen manufacture William moved to the Commercial Sector until his early retirement.

Since then he has resumed watercolour

LaGrange

Nestled serenely amid the rolling, green foothills of the western Piedmont Plateau stands LaGrange, Georgia. The laid-back beauty of the, at first, seemingly sleepy little Southern city belies the network of activities which whirls constantly in this modern, up-to-date capital city of West Georgia. The downtown street plan has not altered since surveyor Samuel Reid laid it out in 1827. The focal point of the town is an elegant park replete with an enormous statue and fountain. The park was originally designed as the home of the courthouse and served as such until 1936. Away from the four corners of the square run the eight principal streets in north-south and east-west directions. This wonderful public area was known as Court Square until 1976, when the statue was placed in the fountain. It is now known as LaFayette Square, for the statue is of the famous French aristocrat in whose honor the town was named.

LaGrange was chartered in December 1828 as the seat of government for the then newly created County of Troup. The whole region had been bought in 1825 from the Creek Nation, all forty-nine of their leading chiefs having signed the sale agreement. The then Governor of Georgia was George M. Troup, for whom the county was named. A community meeting was held about March of 1828 to select a town name. Julius Caesar Alford, later known in history as 'The War Horse of Troup' in Congress, made the suggestion. The name was to honor Marie Joseph Paul Roch Yves Gilbert du Motier, the Marquis de LaFayette. Alford had been among the hosts for LaFayette when he came to Georgia in 1825. Passing through the newly acquired western area, LaFayette had remarked that the countryside was similar to his estate in France, the Chateau of LaGrange-Blenau, forty miles from Paris. LaFayette was a much-loved hero of the American Revolution and a personal friend and advisor to Washington, Jefferson and others. His life was spent in seeking freedom for America, the French people, and finally in anti-slavery work.

The face of LaGrange, as with so many American towns and cities, has changed with regularity over the past 170 plus years. There is just enough preserved though from each time period (in the way of our built environment) that anyone from any point in our history would still find things that were familiar to him, though the whole would be quite different. We have, around the square, newly renovated areas, such as the LaFayette Plaza, home to our Chamber of Commerce. We have buildings from the turn of the century, some from the 1870s, and just two blocks from the square, a house dating to 1828.

Unlike most frontiers, Troup County was settled by people of culture, wealth and accomplishment. The large planters preceded the small farmers. They came to transplant the 'Old Virginian' civilization onto the new land. They brought their institutions and adapted them to the new environment. They came prepared for a rich full life. They brought not only mules for plowing, but fine horses for racing, riding, and fox hunting.

They brought wagons for work and carriages for pleasure and comfort. They brought seed to plant crops but also cuttings of boxwood (an ornamental shrubbery used in gardens and yards) as well as flowers for their formal gardens. They were fond of gardens, and every home boasted its own miniature park of English or Italian style. They brought their Bibles for practical living and the classics for entertainment. They also brought a plethora of slaves, the basis of their great wealth, whose contributions helped make rapid development possible. Pioneer blacks were a skilled and intelligent workforce that included many excellent craftsmen, artisans, laborers and engineers.

The influence of religion was a vital component in the rapid and refined settlement of West Georgia, particularly Troup County. Religious institutions (churches and schools) helped set LaGrange apart from typical 'frontier towns' as well.

LaGrange, in the antebellum era, was one of those few places where the romanticized 'Hollywood' version of the Old South actually existed. Charles H. C. Willingham, local editor, would ever after refer to the halcyon days before 1860 as the period of LaGrange's 'ancient prestige'. LaGrange was where most planters chose to live, rather than on their plantations, though many had homes there, too. Their large holdings created an atypically large upper class as Troup County was the fifth largest slave-holding county in Georgia and fourth wealthiest in terms of taxes.

LaGrange quickly became a hub of commerce and government. It rapidly developed as a center of culture and education. Troup County Academy, for boys, was the first school, in 1828. In 1838, it became LaGrange High School, owned by the city but managed by a Board of Trustees. The trustees hired a principal who earned his living charging tuition. There was at one time a military academy and a male college, known as Brownwood University. Brownwood was founded as a third female college in town but converted to a men's school about 1850. It closed in 1861 when all the young men went off to war. Attempts after 1865 to restart it failed.

The other two female colleges founded in antebellum LaGrange survived into the Twentieth Century. The younger school, Southern Female College, founded in 1842, closed just after World War I largely due to a series of disastrous fires. The other, our only surviving college, received its charter as LaGrange Female Academy in 1831. It became coeducational, officially, in 1952 and today is a main part of the town's life and economy. It has belonged to the Methodist Church Georgia Conference since 1857.

As LaGrange grew and prospered between 1830 and 1860, a great national crisis, between the commercial and agrarian sectors of the nation, came to a head. LaGrange people did not favor leaving the Union, though they understood the Constitutionality of doing so. They did, however support their state when the decision to part was made. As company after company of young men departed from LaGrange's depot, soon followed by increasingly older men, it was clear that LaGrange would be undefended if an emergency arose. A corps of wealthy, young ladies in town determined to form a militia of their own for home defense. They named themselves the 'Nancy Harts' in honor of a Georgia heroine of the American Revolution who successfully defended her home against British soldiers.

During the war the women drilled, marched, practiced and acquired martial training. They also operated the equivalent of a 'USO'. They, and other groups, such as The Electa Club, provided parties, balls, dinners, and plays, some of which they wrote, for soldiers who found themselves in LaGrange enroute to duty, on furlough, or convalescing in one of the several local Confederate hospitals. LaGrange's location in the heart of the Confederate States was a perfect hospital zone, especially since railroads linked it with all three fronts. The threat of actual war was, for a while, far removed. The rails also brought hundreds of refugees, too, who likewise felt the area safer than their homelands.

Great numbers fled to or through LaGrange in search of sanctuary. Most of the highest ranking Confederate officials and Congressmen stayed at one time or another in LaGrange. Many were guests of the Benjamin H. Hills at 'Bellevue'. Jefferson Davis, the Confederate President was frequently feted in LaGrange by a myriad of friends. Confederate Navy Secretary Stephen R. Mallory, was arrested at 'Bellevue' along with Ben Hill in May of 1865 by Union General Upton, who had been detailed to LaGrange for that purpose.

Small raids in 1863 caused a company of older Troup men to begin guarding the Chattahoochee River. Remnants of the Union Army defeated at the Battle of Brown's Mill in neighboring Coweta County were again engaged by local militia under Capt. Sanford H. Dunson at Philpot's Ferry. They were seeking to re-cross the river and rejoin their main army. The Federal Army took West Point, in the southwest corner of Troup County on April 16, 1865 and reached LaGrange the next day. The 'Nancy Harts' met and marched west on Broad Street to intercept them. Coming over the high hill that was the campus of LaGrange Female College, like a blue flood, was a swarm of soldiers. A column of nearly 3000 others came around 'The Hill' led by Union Colonel Oscar H. LaGrange. Ironically he bore the same name as our town. Filled with the terror of a thousand refugee tales, the women stood their ground, determined to save their homes or die trying. Colonel LaGrange was not making war on civilians and gladly exchanged a promise to spare the town's homes for the surrender of the brave women. Colonel LaGrange had heard, first hand, of Benjamin H. Hill's many generous acts towards Northerners seeking for dead or wounded loved ones. The Colonel stopped his army two miles from LaGrange and gave strict orders that the Hill family and their possessions were not to be harmed. Some depredations occurred. Heirlooms and items of value not hastily hidden were purloined. The business district was burned along with all war-support industry (tanyard, tinworks and steam mill). The furniture factory was spared because it was only making coffins by that time. The depot was burned and the railroad destroyed.

In 1888, LaGrange's first cotton mill was built. One at Troup Factory, nine miles from LaGrange, dated to 1848. The manufacturing companies begun in West Point in 1869 had their mills over the state line in Alabama. Textiles boomed and eventually LaGange had nine factories. Most investors were local men, whose capital had been made in commerce and farming. In the days prior to World War I, industrialization led to town expansion, physically and numerically. A public school system opened in 1903. County schools had been operating over thirty years. The public schools in LaGrange soon put the private ones out of business. Dairying became a chief agricultural pursuit and local creameries won international prizes. Two new railroads crossed LaGrange connecting the town with added opportunities. Growth brought other needs: a fire department, street paving, water lines, sewers and electric lights.

LaGrange citizens opposed involvement in World War I. Nevertheless, they responded in the same manner they had in 1861 when they had not favored secession. Once their country was in it they backed it to the hilt. LaGrange contributions to the war effort brought national acclaim. Several local women volunteered to drive ambulances in Paris. Troup County's quota of men (2,367) was exceeded on the first day of registration when 3,226 volunteered. Troup County was noted nation-wide for its war organization and bond drives. In all five Liberty Loan Bond Drives, Troup County not only oversubscribed their quotas everytime, on the first day of the drive, but were first in the United States to do so everytime.

An additional need was for health services. The mills owned and directed by Fuller Callaway had Mission of the Good Shepherd hospital, founded by Callaway with cooperation from the Episcopal church. Joseph E. Dunson, like Callaway, one of the premier textile giants of the town, gave the city money for a public hospital to serve both black and white citizens. Dunson Hospital served until 1939 when it moved to more expansive quarters and was re-named City-County Hospital. It developed into today's West Georgia Medical Center, largely through the enormous generosity of Callaway Foundation. Now in its eighty-fourth year, West Georgia Health System has seven major divisions – the hospital, Florence Hand Home (Nursing Facility), Coleman Health Center, West Georgia Dialysis, a home care unit, a hospice and an assisted living complex.

Things also seemed to be better in LaGrange than in the rest of the country, even during the Great Depression. Our banks closed, but the textile mills survived under the good leadership of Fuller E. Callaway, Jr. and his brother Cason and S. H. Dunson, Jr. and his nephew, Walker S. LaGrange factories were even able to increase pay in the Fall of 1936. Farms were hit hard, but provided for their own needs. Recovery seemed to have come early to LaGrange. There began to be much new building late in the 1930s, all of which was put on hold for World War II.

Again, Troup's people fell into the war with whole hearts. We had sons and daughters at every front. Local groups tracked our young people as they spanned the globe in Europe, Asia, Africa and at home.

Following World War II LaGrange began to expand. One of the greatest factors with the most lasting impact was the 1943 creation of Callaway Foundation Inc.. Its continued contributions elevate the quality of life for all our citizens on a daily basis. Progressive leadership worked to diversify the industrial base in LaGrange. Today our Industrial Park and other areas out from town boast a wide range of industry and business. Textiles continue to lead. Callaway Mills became Milliken and Company; Dixie and Dunson Mills became part of what is now WestPoint Stevens. Both are industry leaders. LaGrange continues to grow and play a vital part in the area's cultural, recreational and educational life.

As the year 2000 approaches we find LaGrange reaching more and more to an international connection. One component of that has been the sister city program. Our first tie was with Aso, Japan in 1979. We added Poti, in the Republic of Georgia in 1990. Our third Sister City is Craigavon, Northern Ireland which brought about the production of this book.

LaGrange is a city of roughly 28,000 people, close to half of the population of the county as a whole. Our economy is diversified and so are the lifestyles of our people. LaGrange has things no other town its size could imagine (art galleries and museums, archives, a symphony, ballet, operatic company and every sport facility imaginable) which even many large American cities do not have. Much of this is owed to a history of dedicated, city leaders and planners. Much is attributable to our heritage of community spirit. The bulk of it is directly a contribution of the Callaway family, the foundations which they created and continue to direct. LaGrange has always been a center of culture, education, beautiful homes and gardens and intelligent people.

Parklands

LaGrange has one of the best-known nature center-resorts in America in neighboring Harris County, Georgia. It started as a woodland retreat or lodge for the Fuller Callaways, but became the principal home of the Cason Callaway family after he left the family textile business in LaGrange. Centered around 'Blue Springs' – the cold side of the mountain from Franklin Roosevelt's famous Warm Springs, it was only natural that Cason and Franklin would become friends.

Cason Callaway first developed a 'model farm' program in the area which soon became a model of work to preserve native plants, enhance preservation of nature and be a resort and education center all in one. Appropriately, Cason Callaway and his wife, Virginia, not only founded this remarkable parkland, but were leaders in building Georgia Hall at Warm

Sibley Horticulture Center at Callaway Gardens

A scenic of Azalea-lined Piney Woods Lake in LaGrange

Springs, which became the centerpiece of the rehabilitation center there. Of course, Roosevelt's 'Little White House' is there too in neighboring Meriwether County, and is itself a peaceful refuge and education center.

Callaway Gardens offers many programs that involve people in horticultural education and appreciation. The gardens, named for Cason's mother, Ida Cason Callaway, boasts hiking and bicycling trails, nature drives, a chapel set deep in the woodland, for meditation; several lakes, the Sibley Horticulture Center and Day Butterfly Center. There is also Mr Cason's Vegetable Garden which is frequently featured on the national television series Victory Garden. There are, additionally, recreation areas with a beach, rides, picnic area and a Circus every summer and a Festival of Lights every Christmastide. Four golf courses make this an ideal place for a PGA tour annual event, the Buick Challenge. The Gardens are also home to the Master's Ski Tournament and a steeplechase every Fall, part of which revenues go to local arts groups. In LaGrange there are several public parks, many of them dedicated to some sport or recreation. Some are city owned, some county and some by the Troup County Parks and Recreation Department. The major ones include Dunson Park, a baseball park; Callaway Stadium for football (American style); and City Park for

Primeval ferns and a modern waterfall – inside the Sibley Center – make for a restful stroll

swimming. Other park areas include LaFayette Square, the center of downtown LaGrange and Union Park located in East LaGrange. The Callaway Memorial Park on the south side of town centers around a ninety-three foot tall clock tower. It was fashioned after the Campanile de San Marco in Venice, Italy. It was built with funds contributed by sorrowing employees of Fuller Callaway, Sr. when he died in 1928 and was completed in 1929. Lake West Point offers many park areas around its 500 miles of shoreline. In times past, people resorted to Hill View Cemetery on Sundays and special times. They passed local and family lore to the next generation as they strolled past the graves of lost loved ones. Music and sometimes speeches were heard from a bandstand built in the midst of the cemetery. The many elegant tombstones made it much like walking through a sculpture gallery as well.

Familiar Flowers and Butterflies

Dogwood

Tiger Swallowtail

Magnolias

Blue Azure

Azalea

Peaches

American Painted Lady

Iris

Cloudless Sulfur

Magnolia

Stately Homes

LaGrange has been, from its earliest days, the location of many stately homes. As the residential center of a wealthy cotton planting society, with its concomitant cultural and social attractions, LaGrange in the 19th century boasted over one hundred Greek Revival style homes, many of imposing proportions. As industry, mainly textile factories, began to dominate the local economy between 1880 and 1900, dozens of large homes in the Victorian style soon dotted the town. Around 1905, a return to interest in Federal, Neoclassical, Georgian, and Tudor styles manifested itself in our new homes, many of which were considered mansions. Many homes of these last two eras have also vanished, mostly due to fires. Stately homes are still being built in LaGrange, the most recent being that of the Emmett Harts.

Some homes still stand from each of our various, identifiable time periods. 'Bellevue' and 'The Oaks' are but two examples of the grand Greek Revival style of the Antebellum Era. 'Bellevue' was home to one of Troup County's most nationally prominent figures, Benjamin Harvey Hill. It was host to most every leader of the Confederate Government, including President Jefferson Davis. It is now the home of the LaGrange Woman's Club, an arrangement made possible by Fuller and Alice Callaway. The best surviving example of Victorian architecture, in the high style known as Queen Anne, is 'In Clover'. Built as a home by the Dallis family it has been adapted for use as a restaurant and now offices. 'Sunny Gables' from the 1920s is the finest remaining English Manor style home. It

Franklin D. Roosevelt's 'Little White House' in Warm Springs, GA.

A Stately Greek-Revival Mansion b— in the 1840s 'The Oaks' on Ver— Road, LaGra—

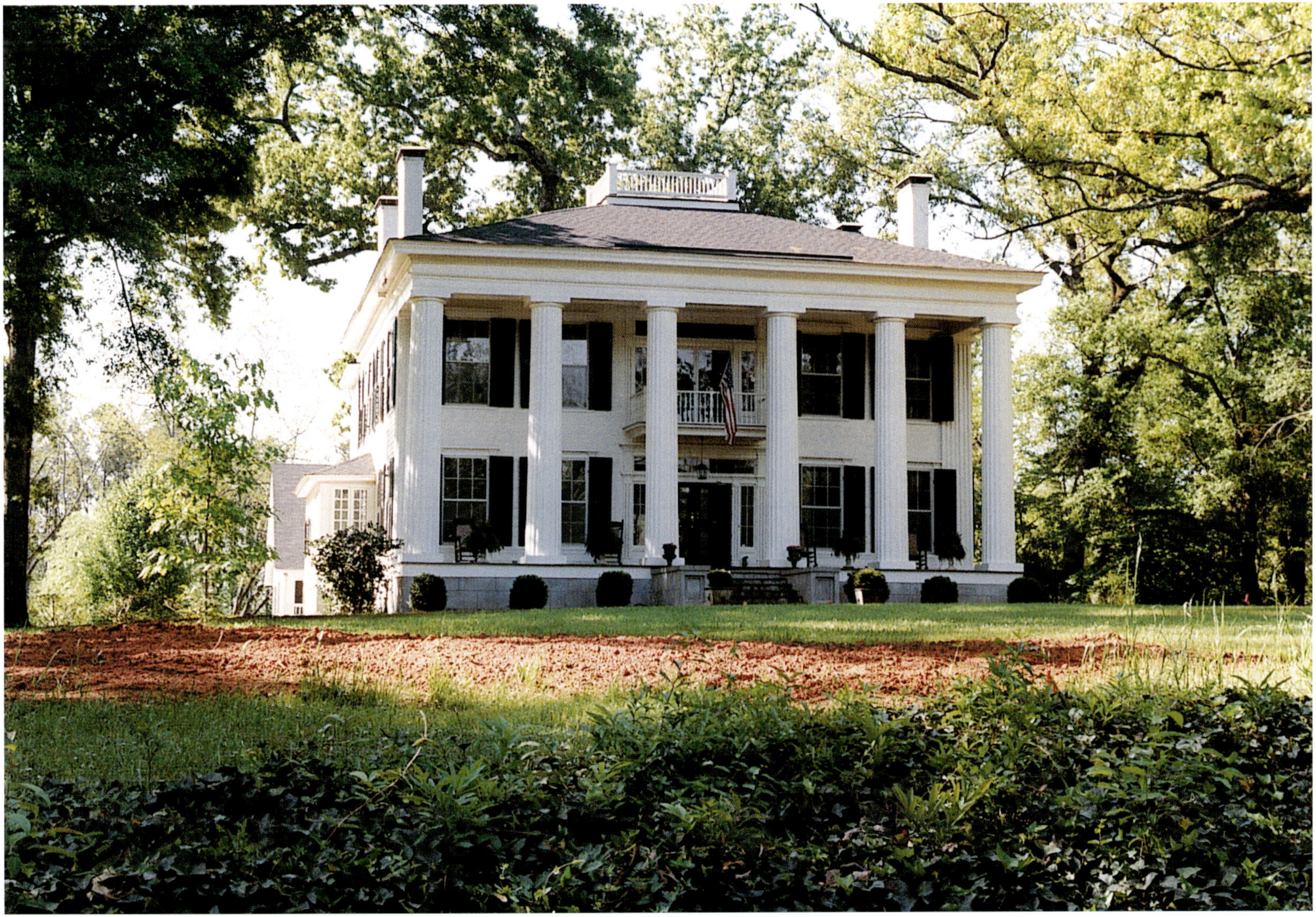

'Bellevue' – home of LaGrange Woman's Club, Built for Benjamin Harvey Hill in the 1850's

is part of LaGrange College, now, and will soon be home to the President and his family. The best surviving stately home is 'Hills and Dales', the Italian Renaissance villa designed by Neil Reid to blend in with the historic formal gardens which came with the place. The gardens featured Italian-style terraces, and were largely created by Sarah Coleman Ferrell as she expanded a garden site her mother created in the 1830s. In 1912, Fuller E. Callaway bought the estate and built the current house. It has distinct Palladian features and an inviting, rounded portico on one end. It has been the scene of many local galas, fund raising parties for local organizations, and of course, Callaway family events. Many national and international celebrities have been entertained here from the International Cotton Convention in 1919 to Ingrid Bergman. 'Hills and Dales' is thus one of the best known LaGrange places in the world.

Restful, elegant, Italian-style 'H. and Dales' home of the Callawa built in 1914-19

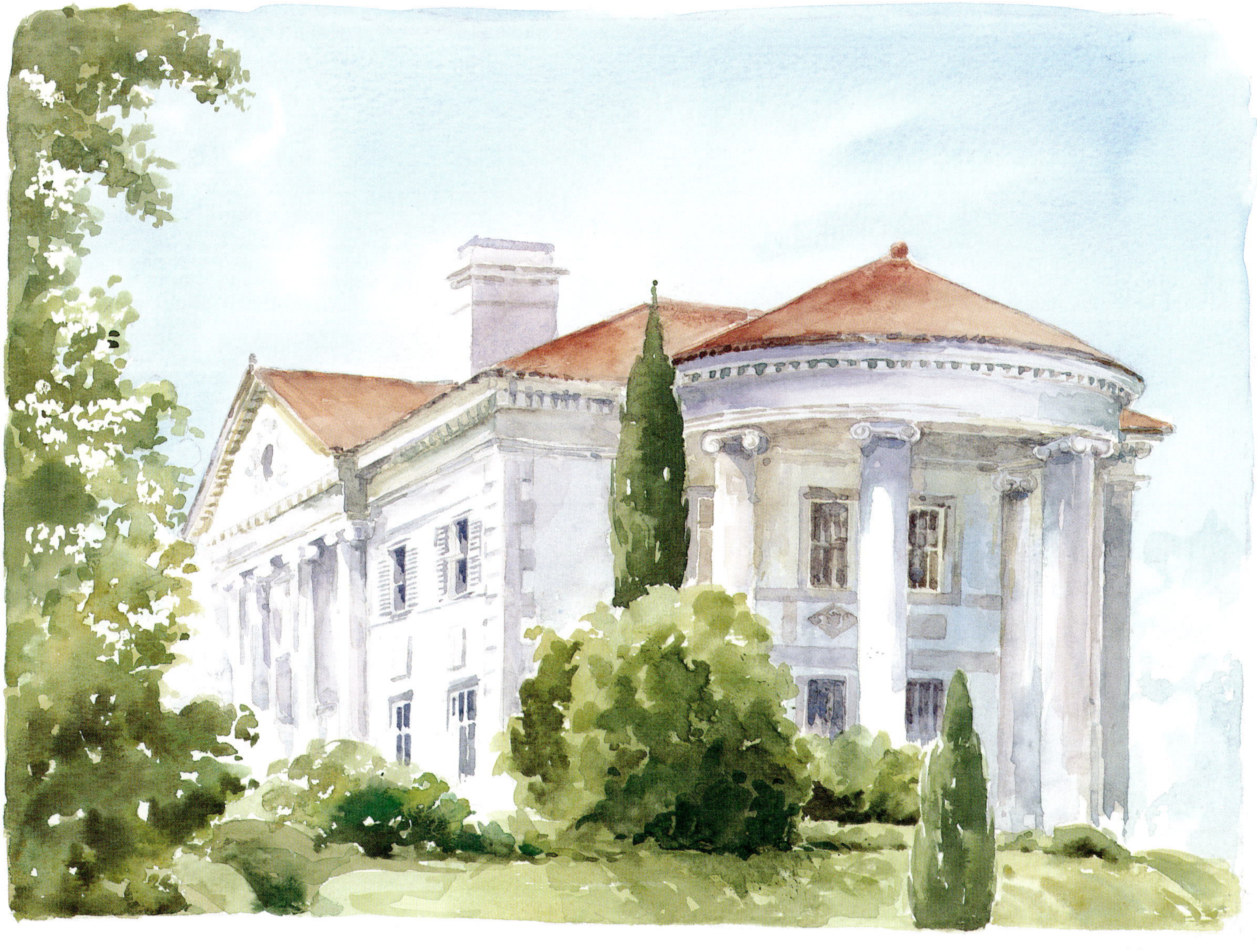

Times Past

Of the over 100 antebellum homes, most of Greek Revival style, found in LaGrange in 1860, less than two dozen have survived. Perhaps as few as another two dozen also remain around the county itself. They often call up stories from long since departed great grandparents. There are, though, a good number of historic homes and structures from later periods still extant. Many have been renovated for adaptive use.

In LaGrange, the Troup County Archives was a three-storied Neo-classical bank built in 1917. Many people still come in the reading room and recall having done some banking transaction or another. "The tellers' counter used to be along that wall" they say, or "Mr Smith's office was right there in that area." The 1892 county jail, a Romanesque style edifice now serves as the home of the Chattahoochee Valley Art Museum.

On Main Street stands the 1912 United States Post Office, a jewel of Georgian-style architecture. Now, only those over middle age still recall the concession and paper stand operated in one corner of the post office by blind Miss Pearl Dozier, who knew everyone in town by the sound of their footfall. The old Davis Pharmacy building is a masterwork of memories and Victorian commercial architecture. Most of the east side of downtown's LaFayette Square recalls the King family, whose patriarch, Horace King, was a freed slave turned master bridge-builder and local architect-builder. He and his sons built most of that block.

The old Coca-Cola Bottling Plant, built in 1940 in Art Moderne style is now offices. It evokes, still, strong memories among 1000s of residents who can remember an annual school trip to the

Jones Cross Roads Store, built of native field stones about 1900 on the southern edge of Troup County

plant to see its fascinating works and receive a free, iced Coke. The classic lines of the pavilion at City Pool recall many summers of youthful fun. Just the sight of it, in passing, can cool one off on a hot day. The Italianate designed facade of the old LaGrange Theatre cannot help but take one back to a Saturday morning matinee with dozens of children munching (and throwing) popcorn or that first date in the dark balcony on the eve of adolescence.

An old boxed well with pulley and bucket from a simpler day and age

An Antebellum farmhouse with an added Victorian portico in neighbouring Meriwether County, GA

The old general store and post office at Stovall, GA.

Cannon at restored Ft. Tyler in West Point

*Flowers
and foliage growing
over picket fences is a nostalgic link with
our heritage that still we find, now and then, along the roads and streets.*

The remaining old textile mills, still partially surrounded by their former 'villages' bring to mind a simpler, small-town era. A stroll down Broad Street, with some of its trees still towering over the road and its few remaining grand mansions, brings back a day when most of the streets leading away from the square were similarly elegant and beautiful.

Cumbee's Old General Store in Chambers Co., Alabama just over the State line from us.

This Plantation hous was among the earlie Troup County homes Its 'Story and a Half style was a familiar site around our area

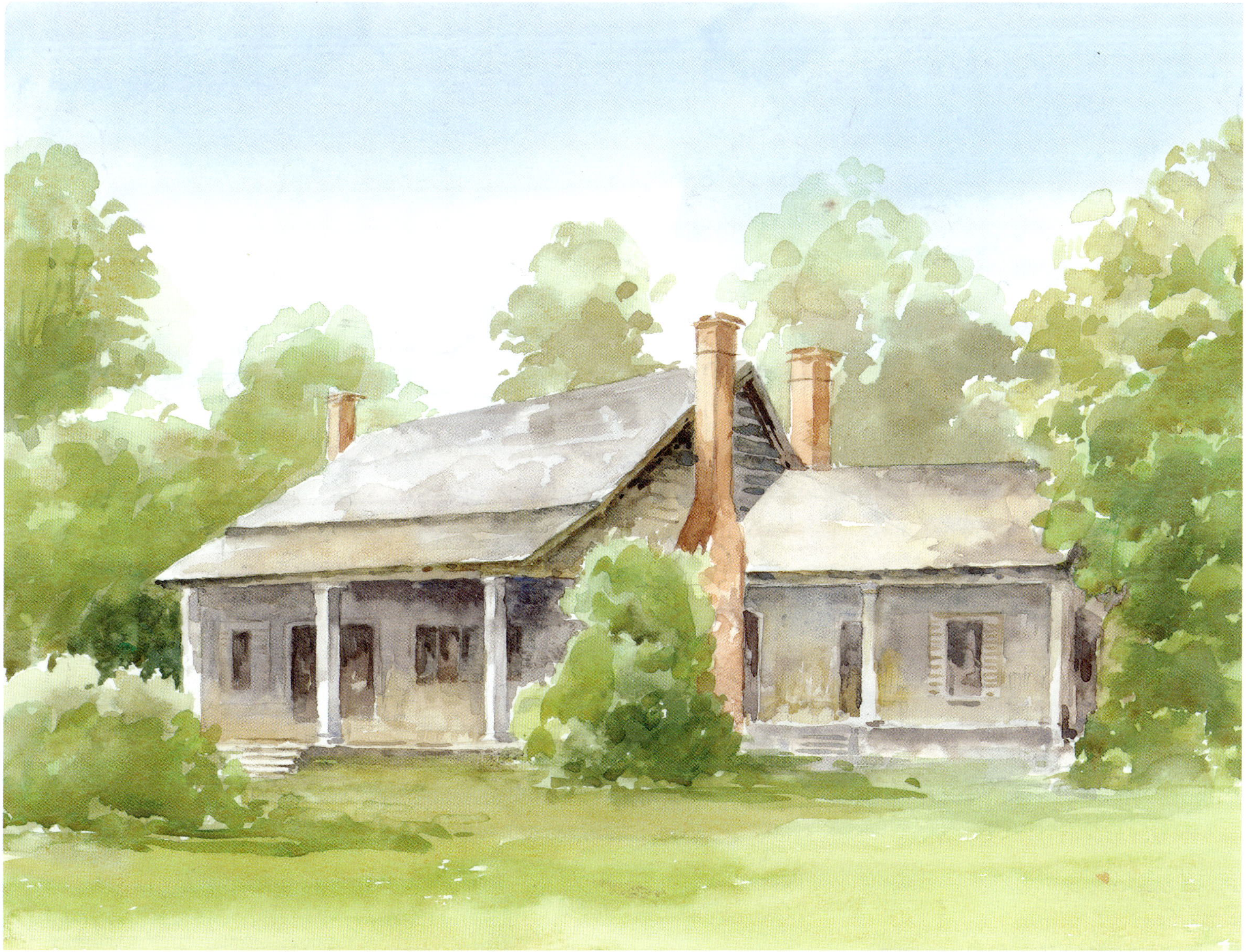

Arts and Crafts

LaGrange is a cultural center. There are opportunities for expression of every form of art, music and performance. In the nineteenth century the several colleges which flourished in LaGrange were a main source of cultural activity. Their music and art departments were premier. Concerts, theatricals, and touring shows came to LaGrange, as did bands and circus troops. Lectures of public interest and balls, military parades, and public suppers were frequent. Besides the college auditoriums, performances were often held in church buildings, the courthouse and at Sterling Hall, later renamed Truitt Opera House.

Today LaGrange College offers cultural and educational opportunities unequalled in most communities our size, centered around the Lamar Dodd Art Center, Price Theatre and Callaway Auditorium. The latter is home of the annual Azalea Story-Telling Festival, co-sponsored by the college, Troup County Schools and Memorial Library. LaGrange has a ballet company, a symphony orchestra, two art museums and several art organizations and professional-level vocal performing groups for adults and youth. The music and drama departments of LaGrange College as well as the high schools chorus and drama classes combine to offer some form of performance all through the year.

The LaGrange Symphony Orchestra was founded in the 1980s with assistance from LaGrange College. They give several classical concerts during the September through May season and a Christmas concert, Youth concert and provide programs in the schools. They also sponsor a Young Artist Competition. The LaFayette Society for Performing Arts is an umbrella group

Above: Chattahoochee Valley Art Museum in LaGrange. Below: Lamar Dodd Art Center at LaGrange College

for several others. The adult LaFayette Chorale gives semiannual concerts. The Young Singers of LaGrange, a youth choir, does local concerts and has performed in New York City. They plan to participate in an International Youth Choir Festival in Canterbury, England in the year 2000. The LaGrange Ballet has junior and senior divisions and professionally taught classes and performances.

The Chattahoochee Valley Art Association was founded in 1963. Later, its last name changed to 'Museum'. It offers art classes, annual Arts and Crafts Fairs and juried national art competitions as well as operating an 8,700 square foot museum in an 1892 building renovated and donated to them by Callaway Foundation. LaGrange College also has a museum, named for LaGrange's internationally renowned artist, Lamar Dodd. It, too, was donated by Callaway Foundation Inc.

The Troup County Historical Society promotes local preservation, history education and research as well as maintaining many local records. It also publishes works on local history. The Society also operates the Troup County Archives in a 1917 built bank, provided by Callaway Foundation.

An old time street scene preserved at Warm Springs

Annie Greene, one of Lagrange's hometown artists with a special flair she developed called 'String Art'

Leisure and Recreation

Serene Scene on beautiful West Point Lake

LaGrange is a mecca for every type and variety of leisure activity. Lake West Point covering its 26,000 acres of the county's once best farmlands is home to one of America's best Largemouth Bass lakes. Fishing and boating are supplemented around the 500 miles of shoreline by parks, campsites and barbeque grills. There are beaches and marinas too.

Recreation facilities, in addition to those for organized sports are all around. There are tracks, playgrounds, water parks and pools in all sections of the town for one's freetime use. Our older citizens have a special place, the Senior Center, where they can gather for meals, dancing, classes, bridge games or television in a 12,000 square foot facility. Trips and other events are organized for them there.

There is a Wild Animal Park just south

Golf is among the chief sports and recreation activities year-round

Two re-enactors relive authentic military life of the war between the States inside rebuilt Ft. Tyler on the Georgia – Alabama line

of LaGrange, enroute to Callaway Gardens that has guided and self-drive tours. The animals, from every continent, add an educational component to this leisure time activity. Close to it is a re-created corn mill and family entertainment center, Butts Mill Farm, which offers a look into life in the last century.

Nearly any leisure activity one can imagine could be pursued in LaGrange. There are all sorts of clubs, based on one's interests. There are many civic/service clubs such as Rotary, Lions and Kiwanis. There are women's organizations, such as Women's Club and Pilot Club. Some groups are organized around some historic event, such as the American Revolution or the War Between the States. The latter includes groups of people who like to dress in historic costumes and 're-enact' specific battles. One group, mostly of people from out of town, annually gathers to 're-enact' the fall of Fort Tyler in nearby West Point, Georgia. It was the last Confederate fort to fall in the war, on Easter Sunday, April 16, 1865. Some groups are composed of people wanting to celebrate their ethnic heritage. The Order of the Tartan is a group of locals who share their Scottish heritage in monthly meetings and annual dinners to honor St Andrew and Robert Burns.

No one need ever be bored around LaGrange.

A few of the many sports available in and around LaGrange

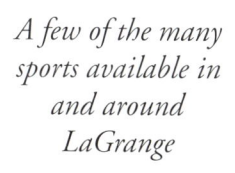

Churches

The first three denominations to establish churches in Troup County remain its principal ones today. These are the Methodist, Presbyterian, and Baptist churches. All three of them have British origins. Presbyterianism is directly from the Church of Scotland, Methodism is a branch from the Church of England, and an English-born minister, Roger Williams, founded the Baptist Church.

The first church in the county, First Methodist Church of LaGrange, was built in 1827 on the same site it still occupies, though it is now in its fifth sanctuary. The original structure was a hewn-log meeting house. The second church, First Baptist, was founded shortly afterwards, in 1828, and it was followed by First Presbyterian in 1829. These three churches were the only ones in the county seat until the 1860s. Refugees from New Orleans during the War Between the States joined with some local Methodists to create an Episcopal Church, St Marks, in 1864. There were other religions represented in early LaGrange, and the county, but without sufficient numbers to have formal congregations in LaGrange.

The Disciples of Christ and Universalists had churches in Troup County. Many Catholics, mostly Irish, held services in their homes whenever priests from larger cities could be procured, or whenever one was visiting in the area. An increase in Catholic families around World War I, largely of Lebanese extraction, eventually led to the building of St. Peter's Catholic Church in 1936. Since 1970, more and more Catholics have moved to LaGrange in the wake of industrialization. The need arose for a larger church and a new St. Peter's was finished in 1988.

The Marquis de Lafette holds aloft his symbolic cocade in the main square of LaGrange with First Baptist Church in the background

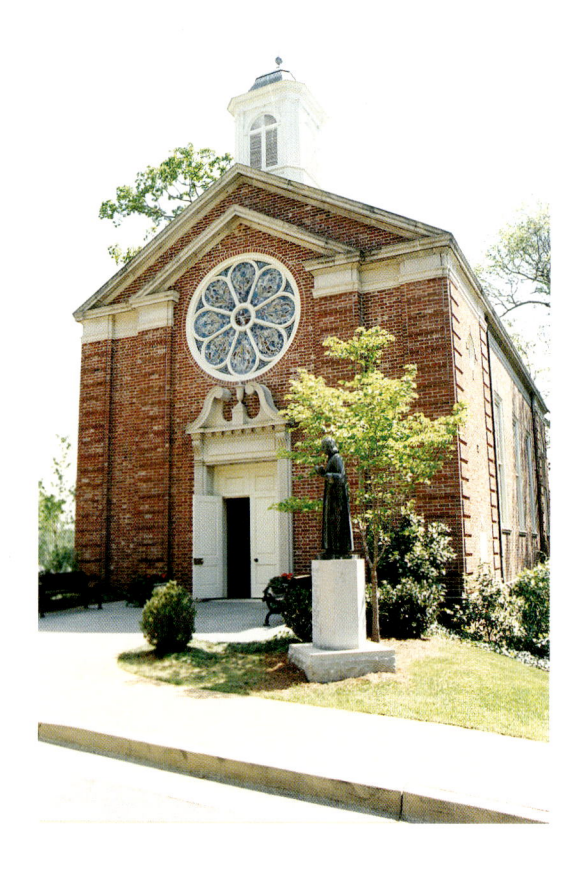

Statue of John Wesley outside LaGrange College Chapel on the Campus. The stained glass came from the old First Methodist Church and dates to 1898.

Ida Cason Callaway Chapel at Callaway Gardens

The old Presbyterian Church in Mountville, Georgia, now a private home

Many Jewish families, mostly of German extraction, made their homes in LaGrange and neighboring West Point from the 1850s on. An increase in the Jewish population eventually led to the establishment of Temple Beth-el in LaGrange and a Jewish Center in 1945.

Our churches have always been a source of community spirit. The various denominations work together harmoniously to celebrate important community, social, and religious events. They cooperate to help run clothing centers, food closets, summer camps, and personal aid agencies.

Our churches do more than look after the spiritual needs of their flocks. They help raise good, substantial citizens, regardless of creed. Our churches are also part of our town's physical attraction with the many beautiful sanctuaries and meeting houses which dot every neighborhood of the city.

Clockwise from top: Welcoming sign, Callaway Gardens: The gate, erected by Alice Callaway, in Ferrall Gardens: some of the boxwood in Ferrall Gardens

Urban and Civic Life

LaFayette

The core, or original center of many American cities has died or decayed. LaGrange is fortunate that good leadership, planning and community support have done much to keep the downtown alive. As in most American cities, fewer people live downtown as subdivisions develop increasingly further out and malls and shopping centers draw business away. Good roads and easy access to individual transportation make this possible. An award winning Main Street Program, among the best in Georgia, has helped LaGrange. An active Downtown Development Authority often in concert with the Troup County Historical Society, and a well-run Chamber of Commerce all contribute to our success. There are few vacant stores in downtown. Many companies operate in restored buildings. Continued renovations of the principal streets and LaFayette Square (heart of downtown) have kept the area attractive. The town fountain, with its statute of the Marquis who our town's name honors, is among our best landmarks. The anchor stores, downtown are mostly locally owned, not chains, and cater to a variety of needs from fashions, furniture, and food to antiques, jewellery and services including a research library and art museum. Downtown is still a place that attracts shoppers, lunchers, and tourists. It is as safe a place for an evening stroll as it was 100 years ago. The 'best burgers in the world' can be found as can elegant luncheons. One local restaurant and shop inhabits a renovated string of structures saved from demolition. They include an 1840s home, 1830s office, and an 1892 sanctuary. Realty, insurance, barbering and novelty shops as well as an art gallery 'On The Square' add to the mix. Most anything one needs can still be found downtown.

"Charlie Joseph's", founded in 1920 is LaGrange's oldest, best-loved hamburger and hotdoggery.

North side LaFayette Square in LaGra

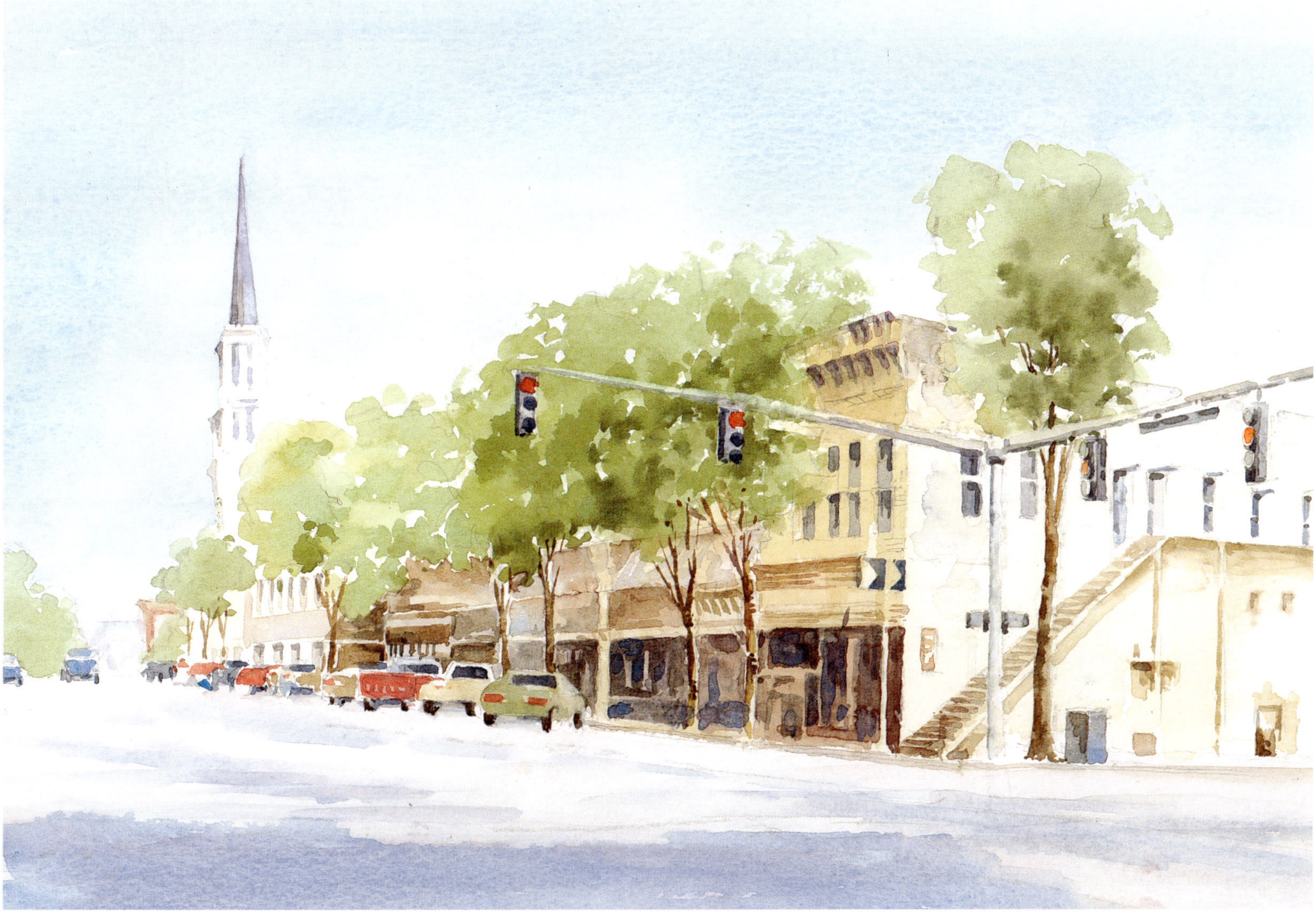

1. *LaFayette Plaza – home of the LaGrange-Troup County Chamber of Commerce.*
2. *City Hall, LaGrange*
3. *Old Theatre – soon to be a civic center*
4. *Troup County Courthouse*
5. *Modern Fire fighting equipment in front of one of our several water towers.*
6. *Victorian Store on Bull Street, LaGrange*
7. *The Troop County Archives, Housed in a 1917 built bank building.*

1.

2.

3.

4.

5.

6.

7.

Commerce Avenue LaGrange, as its na implies, is a hu business acti

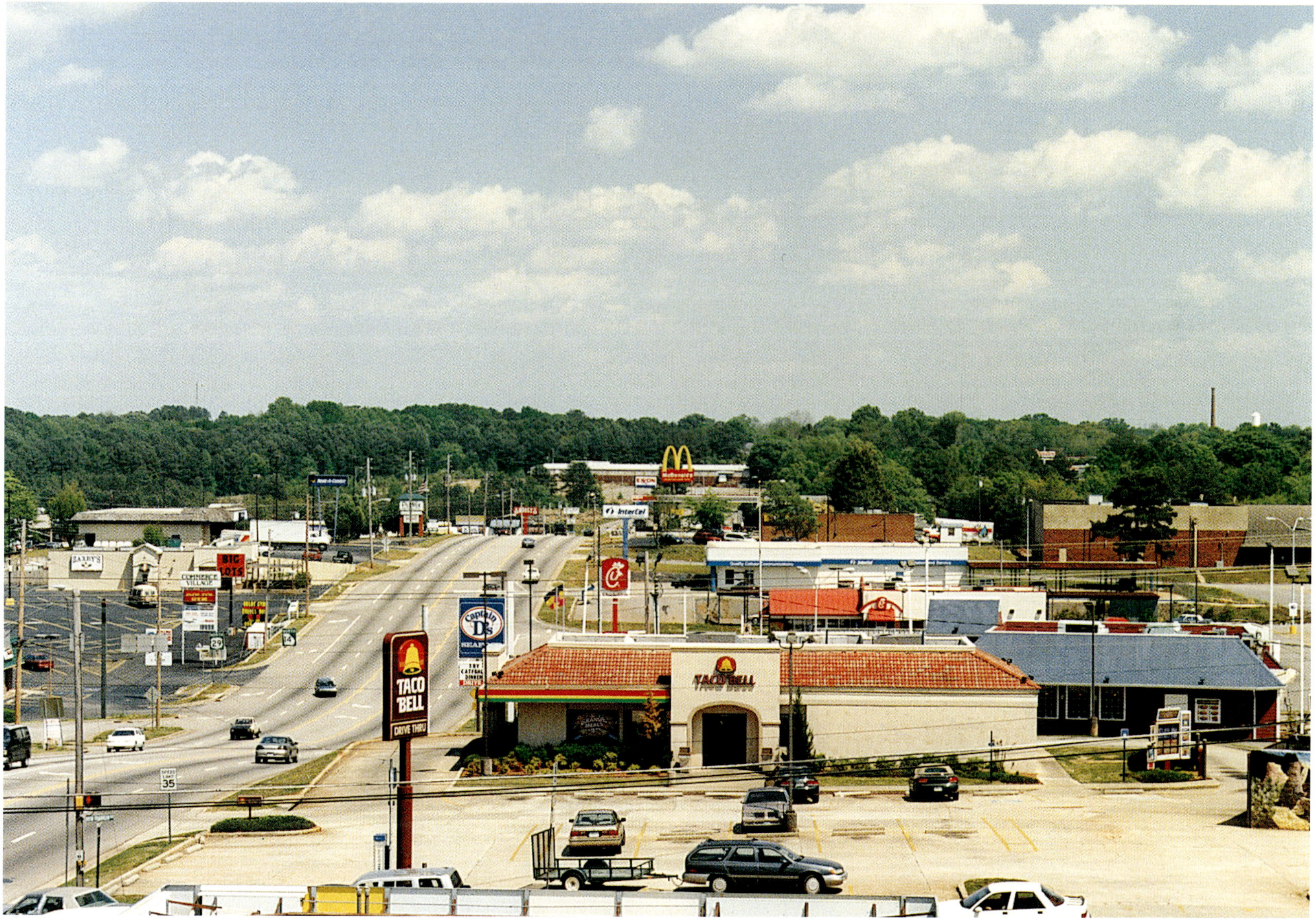

Countryside

When the area around LaGrange first opened for settlement in 1827, it was filled with ancient hardwood forests and deep, rich soil. The Chattachoochee River and several main tributaries flow across the county. They, and a network of smaller streams, increase fertility. Our clayish, red earth banks along the roads, which easily darkens and turns to mud in rain, is one of the sights we hold precious.

Grains of all kinds flourish and initially supported herds of cattle, sheep and swine. Dairying is still a major agricultural pursuit in Troup County. The climate is temperate. Pockets of granite exist. There are also amethyst, tourmaline and a trace of gold found in our soil along with quartz and beryl.

A long time ago, herds of buffalo extended this far east, but the Indians had depleted them long before Europeans arrived. Still, herds of deer are so prevalent as to actually constitute a nuisance in LaGrange as well as through the countryside. Other wild animals still roaming the area include bobcats, panthers and coyotes.

Beavers are fairly common as are racoons and opossum. In recent years, we have begun to see armadillos migrating into our area. Many species of beautiful birds and butterflies call

Abandoned far houses often recall o more agrarian cultu as well as providing scenic landscap

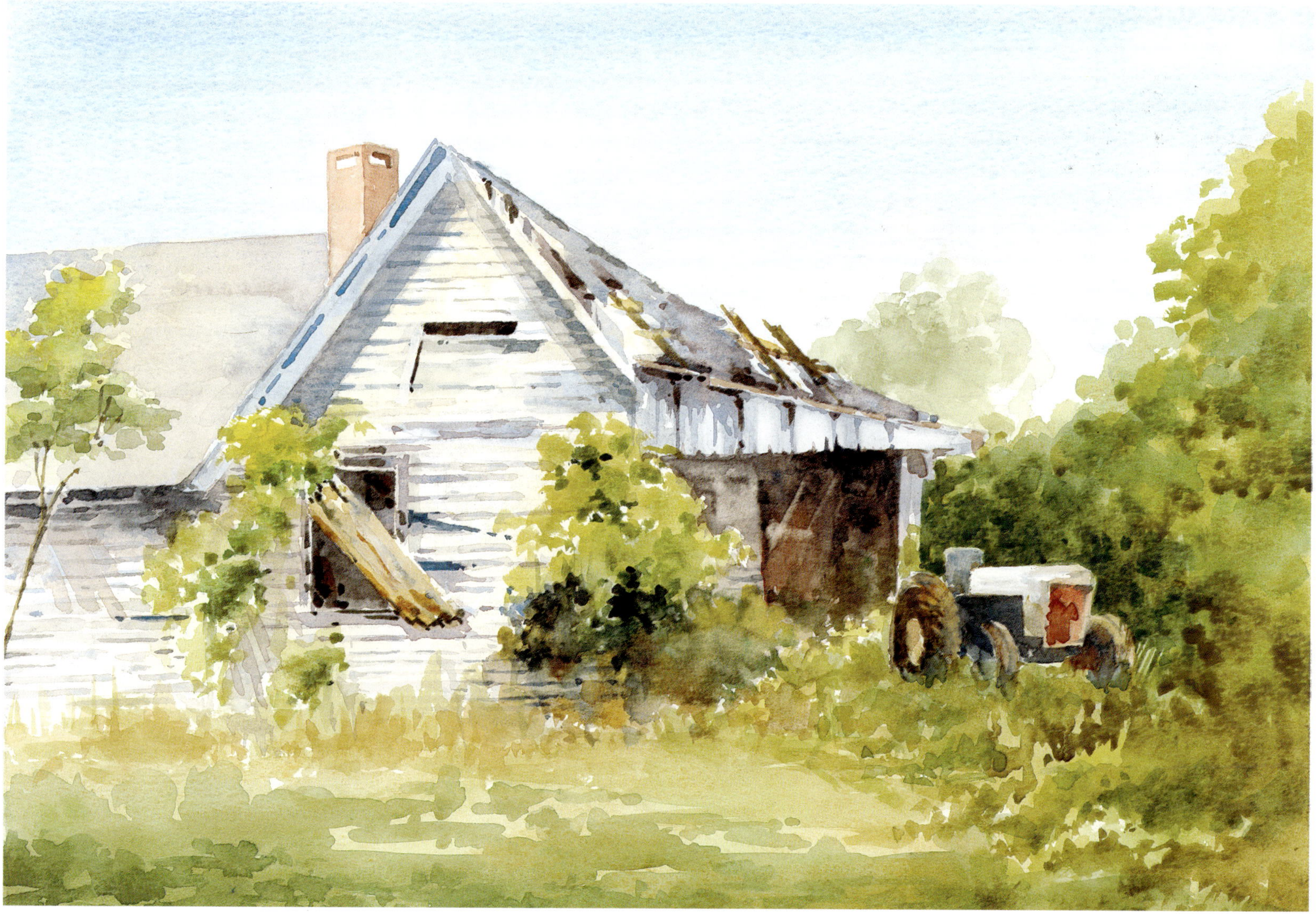

America Redstart

Eastern Bluebird

American Goldfinch

Blue Capped Chickadee

Ruby Throated Hummingbird

Birds often seen in our yards, gardens and wooded areas

this land home. Most any tree, shrub or flower will grow here. Our most popular, locally cultivated plants include: Dogwood, Magnolia, Azalea, Camellia, Roses, Oaks, Pines, Mimosa and Boxwood. Hydrangeas, always popular, are being promoted to heighten interest in an annual festival centered around them. Pecans and peaches are standard crops. The first pecans were brought to Troup County from Texas. One of the largest, early peach orchards operated in the South was in Troup County and neighboring Chambers County, Alabama. It was owned and operated by John H. Parnell, brother of the famed Irish national patriot, Charles Stuart Parnell, who was a Member of Parliament. Despite urban growth and expansion, Troup County still boasts miles and miles of pasture and woodlands. Timber-related businesses are plentiful and profitable. Kudzu, a ground cover imported from Japan, often covers vast acreage along our rural roadsides creating fanciful, artistic shapes.

A winter's supply of firewood, the old well, and some rural mail delivery boxes are still well-known sights in Troup County, though the first two are maintained more from choice than necessity.

Robert Curran's LaGrange

It may be a 'Little White House' but it left a big impression. My step through the door was a step back in time. Everything sits in its original place except for the President himself! Franklin Delano Roosevelt found solace here in 1924 and you could see why. I found a welcome as warm as the springs. The modest presidential holiday home is shrouded in history. He had hoped the natural setting of Pine Mountain would improve his health and it did. The contact with local farmers improved his understanding of their difficulties during the Depression. The haunting image of a wheelchair provides an insight into his battle with paralysis from polio. But the unfinished portrait best sums up a place that has never moved on from the memory of one man.

William McCarroll's LaGrange

It had been a long, uncomfortable journey to Georgia. Since before daylight I had been surrounded by the noise and bustle of strangers - an unsettling experience. Everything was impersonal and anonymous until that evening when I sat on Piney Woods Lake to watch the sunset. A sense of well being and peace suddenly came over me. The crowds and tension were gone. Here, everything was serenity.

The light faded over the lake; the only sounds were from the birds and animals in the forest, the occasional splash of a fish breaking the surface of the lake and the water lapping against the sides of the boat. The evening air hung heavy with the perfume of pine trees and exotic flowers. The fresh greens and silvers were melting into a monochrome as the shadows lengthened. It was a soft and humid evening.

This was the America I had come to see: an expanse of natural beauty and timeless tranquillity. It was to be the first of many beautiful vistas, some of which I have reproduced in my paintings in this book. I have tried to portray the beauty and variety of the scenery in and around LaGrange. I hope my work gives you as much pleasure as it has given me.

Building Bridges that Link our Hearts - Oceans Apart

Some members of the LIFE Executive Board Back row (l to r): Steve Hashimoto, Alex Kalinin, Charles Brachel, Don Lee, Kei Kawata.
Front row (l to r): Gene Woodal, Jan Evans, Margaret Ross (President of LIFE Committee), Bob Walters, Ginger Odum

BLESSED! Indeed! are the citizens of LaGrange, Georgia-America's Greatest Little City. "I live in LaGrange-America's Greatest Little City" was the slogan suggested by a chairman of the LaGrange/Troup County Chamber of Commerce. It caught on and we used it on bumper stickers, stationery, caps, aprons –everywhere! Some of the "greatest" comes from the concept of the sisterhood of cities. It was inaugurated by the President of the United States in 1956 to establish greater friendship and understanding between the people of the United States and other nations, through the medium of direct personal contact: "winning the world to peace one friendship at a time". Spurred by the location of a Japanese owned manufacturing facility – NOK – ,the City of LaGrange became a Sister City with Aso, Kumamoto, Japan on March 13, 1979. Twenty years later many bridges still connect our hearts –oceans apart especially the beautiful gifts of friendship with Mayor and Mrs. Atsuo Kawaski, Yoko Morita, Mr Yamauchi-son, James Satow, Mihoko Shin, Harry Toda, "Indy", Kei "Whatever" Kawata, and the loving Takashi Yamano Family. An exchange between a Tiblisi, Georgia,

USSR television journalist and an American journalist from Atlanta, Georgia prompted the Sister City Relationship with Poti, Georgia, a part of the former USSR. The two journalists attended the Sweet Land of Liberty Parade for Youth in LaGrange and were so moved by the patriotism of the young people and the friendliness of the citizens of LaGrange they thought it would be a perfect match. A step was taken toward world peace through learning about our sister city, loving the people, and having them love us in return. They came and visited us in April, 1990 and the relationship was established. On a return trip to their city by twenty of our citizens, their reciprocity was amazing. They feted us with wine, food, and song by opening their homes and hearts to us. Their adults and children sang, danced, and hung banners in their city to welcome the American Georgians. Many of them could not speak our language, but we soon learned that a smile goes a long way and LOVE eventually wins all. Giorgi Kukhaleshivili was a recipient of that love and friendship when he came as a patient diagnosed with a heart problem in Moscow only to find in LaGrange by a benevolent physician it was not heart related at all, but was a duodenol ulcer; another young man was fitted with an artificial prothesis so that he could return to his native Georgia, marry his childhood sweetheart, and have a beautiful son. We have sent many cargoes of humanitarian aid to a people who so desperately need EVERYTHING! And so more bridges were built and continue to be built, this time an ocean apart in the other Georgia. Now! with sister cities in Aso and Poti the formation of an organization to oversee the Sister City Program for LaGrange was needed. LaGrange City Council approved the "birth" of the LaGrange International Friendship Exchange-[LIFE]. Various volunteers from around the community were asked to serve on LIFE with the mission statement that reads: "To promote peace and understanding between the citizens of LaGrange/Troup County and those of similar communities in other nations through meaningful, lasting exchanges of people, ideas, and cultures". Horizons were expanded for the citizens of LaGrange through new and interesting activities of the two Sister Cities and we were learning how to partner with our distant sisters. LIFE and the city of LaGrange extended an invitation to Craigavon, Northern Ireland to become our third Sister City in March 1996. What a match that has been! They speak our language! and we found that we have so-o-o much in common. After numerous exchanges we are on a solid foundation of admiration, love, and far too many wondrous friendships to acknowledge but these especially: the huggable Chair of SCI –Councillor Kenneth Twyble; the other "M' –Myrtle Porter; –the undauntable Lewis Porter; –the artiste extraordinaire Billy McCarroll; –the witty Robert Curran; the highly esteemed The Honorable David Trimble; –the effervescent SIC Cathy McShane; –beautiful Liz Hamiliton; –gorgeous Caitrionia Hughes; –capable Sharon Magee; –wonderful Trevor Reaney; –sincere Mervyn Carrick; All!! the friends in Craigavon who have touched and helped shape us to be better humans because they love us. The rippling effect of this friendship has touched neighboring Armagh and we have been blessed with music from the gifted organist Baron George Minne at Saint Patrick's Cathedral, the lovely Eithne McGinley and Phillip Donnelly, master glass cutter at Tyrone Crystal who were instrumental in helping a "Craigavon Vase" come into existence. AND! To every member of my beloved LIFE Committee and the citizenery of LaGrange who have been blessed to hear, hug, and experience these gorgeous folk who come to visit us from across the ocean, for we are but a total of the many people we've met because they are friends we could NEVER forget. We have

Craigavon Sister City International & LaGrange International Friendship Exchange

—Building Bridges That Connect Out Hearts-Oceans Apart

open to all Craigavon artists and photographers, William McCarroll, from Lurgan, and Robert Curran, from Portadown, were chosen to travel to LaGrange to capture, on canvas and film respectively, their impressions of their Sister City. In return Alex Kalinin and John Lawrence travelled to Craigavon from LaGrange to carry out a similar task. The fruits of their labours are recorded throughout this book. It is hoped that this publication, which is quite unique in covering two Sister Cities, will not only serve as a pictorial record or to inform the reader through the narrative on the areas concerned, but also act as a catalyst for further contacts and links across the Atlantic.

Lewis Porter

taught each other how to HUG, laugh, cry, learn, work, worship, play, and combine our efforts toward world peace –a peace that can be established one friendship at a time through learning about and loving people of other cultures. We long for business contacts but that is a drop in the bucket when compared to world peace! My prayer is that your life may be blessed by this publication and that you might want to join us on whichever side of the ocean that you happen to reside to help us build bridges that connect our hearts. What a rare privilege and extreme blessing to be able to say, "Many, many thanks, God's blessings, ya'll come and let us together build more bridges!

Margaret Ross

–Building Bridges That Connect Our Hearts-Oceans Apart

LaGrange International Friendship Exchange & Craigavon Sister City International

The SCI and LIFE Committees believe there is a lot more potential to be tapped from the linkage and are constantly on the lookout for other opportunities to exploit the benefits. This book is just one of the ways they plan to get the message across to people and encourage their involvement in the work of helping to broaden the horizons of the citizens of Craigavon and LaGrange in an ever shrinking world. Following a competition exporting, importing, franchising etc have been explored with companies on both sides of the Atlantic.

moved from LaGrange to live in Craigavon. That, together with the fact that Interface Flooring Systems has a plant in Lurgan and its parent plant in LaGrange, ensured there was a 'welcome on the mat' for the visiting delegation. It was truly a case of 'love at first sight' and the bonds of friendship have continued to grow stronger over the subsequent years.

Following an initial 'courtship' the relationship was formalised when in March 1996, Craigavon Borough Council accepted the 'proposal' of LaGrange City Council to become its Sister City. President Dwight D Eisenhower inaugurated the Sister Cities International Programme in 1956 with the following aims: -

– To develop partnerships between US towns, cities, counties and states and similar jurisdictions of other nations;

– To create opportunities for all people to experience and explore other cultures through long-term partnerships;

The Sister City International (SCI) Committee was established in August 1996 with representatives from Local Government, Youth, Medical, Industry, Education, Travel, Tourism and Media who have worked in unison to bring the benefits of the linkage to as broad a spectrum of the citizens of the Borough as possible.

– To create an atmosphere in which economic development and trade can be explored, implemented and strengthened;

– To open dialogue and address issues ranging from the cultural to the technical, from the municipal to the medical, from the environmental to the educational and beyond;

– To stimulate environments through which partnerships can creatively learn, work, and solve problems together;

– To collaborate with other organisations, both in the United States and in other countries, that have similar visions and goals.

We have been greatly assisted by the LaGrange International Friendship Exchange and the City of LaGrange Council. Craigavon's first Honorary Citizens have come from LaGrange in recognition of the role they have played in benefiting the Borough – Don Lee, former Senior Vice-President of Interface; Joe Maltese, Director of Community & Economic Development – LaGrange City Council and Margaret Ross, the indefatigable President of the LIFE Committee.

Projects to date have included a number of school exchanges, golf tournaments, a work experience/educational project under the International Fund for Ireland's Wider Horizons Programme, an exchange of artists and photographers, Civic Leaders exchange, visits by Professors of Art and Drama, a tour by the South Ulster Youth Band and many more visits by private individuals. There has also been an exchange of information on industrial products, public amenities such as Natural Gas, CCTV, waste management, and opportunities for

Sister City International Linkage
– born and nurtured in friendship

Sister City International Committee
Back Row (l to r): Trevor Reaney, Ronnie McCoo, Brian Courtney, Osmond Mulligan.
Front Row (l to r): Lewis Porter, Caitríona Hughes, Councillor Kenneth Twyble, Cathy McShane, Mitchell Graham
Not available for photograph: Sean Hughes

When you enter the Borough of Craigavon you will see on the Borough signage the legend – 'Sister City of LaGrange, Georgia, USA' but are you aware of what lies behind those few words? Read on and you will glean something of their significance. The purpose of this book is to promote not only the individual areas of Craigavon and LaGrange but also to celebrate and make more people aware of the links that exist between them.

When Craigavon Borough Council's Economic Development Committee decided to 'Go West' in 1993, a number of locations were visited in the USA in an endeavour to find a suitable city with which to establish links. Due to the Ulster-Scots connection it was decided to look to the Southern States. LaGrange, Georgia was included in the itinerary for the exploratory visit at very short notice through a personal friendship with someone who had

Alex Kalinin's Craigavon

My first day in Craigavon is to be remembered. Many years back when I lived in England I always yearned to visit and get to know Ireland .... but lack of time never gave me this pleasure. But now here I was!

All of my friends who had visited there a week or two prior to my turn had warned that the weather would be cold and most probably drizzling. Thus I had taken precautions by packing all the proper clothing.

As if by some Heavenly arrangement and power, the skys above revealed their welcoming bright blue colour and sunlighted hills, fields and towns. In fact nine of my ten days were thus. Most of all it brought people into that good humoured Spring-like mood......prams with babies, chatting neighbours, smiling faces everywhere.

Bowlers at Portadown Bowling Green

John Lawrence's Craigavon

What was most appealing and obvious to me of my impressions of Northern Ireland is the love and care the people of Northern Ireland have for their land and country. This was evident in the wonderfully maintained gardens, farms and villages that we visited in the short time that I was there. Of the many photographs that I made, my favorites are the portraits of the craftsmen that we met.

Wherever one goes in Northern Ireland one is aware of the hand of man. The landscape reminds one of a patched quilt. It seemed that every square inch of land is put to good use – from narrow roads lined with walls to open rolling green pastures, the presence of man and his desire to create is apparent, often even in the designs of the stone masonry and metal gates. As a photographer, I hope my craft is not just pictorial. In my work I would also like to convey the spirit of a place and people. In a sense, I think these photographs represent more than just men who make things with natural materials, they also mirror the love of land, hard work, harmony and creation.

Traditional Woodworker

Apple Orchard, Birches

Kinnego Marina, Lough Neagh

Golf/Ski Centre

Master McGrath

sporting interest with great rivalry between Portadown Football Club and Lurgan based Glenavon in the Irish League. Other sports provided for include hockey, with several Astroturf pitches being available in Portadown and Brownlow, tennis, Gaelic Athletic Association sports, karting and archery.

Fishing also features largely in the Borough with Lough Neagh and the River Bann catchment offering some of the finest coarse fishing in Western Europe. If you want to hook perch, bream, roach, rudd and pike or trout this is the place to come.

If on the other hand it is fine feathers you are interested in then the Lough Neagh Discovery Centre is definitely the place to visit where a world of wonder awaits. Situated in the Oxford Island National Nature Reserve the Discovery Centre has won a

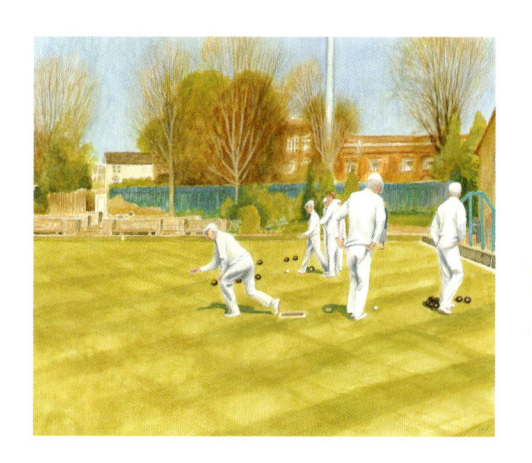

Portadown Bowling Green

number of major awards. It has viewing windows overlooking the waters and reedbeds of the Lough and is connected to the shore by a wooden bridge. The Centre interprets the history and ecology of the Lough through exhibitions, audiovisual shows, interactive computers and games.

Fishing from the Bann Boulevard, Portadown

Churches

Quaker graveyard, Lynastown

When John Wesley, the founder of Methodism, visited Portadown in the 18th Century he described it as a town 'not troubled by much religion.' However Christianity has had an impact on the area for a considerable period of history. Seagoe Parish on the east of the Bann in Portadown, for example, dates back to 500 or 600AD when St. Patrick was said to have been there. The ruins of the old Seagoe Church can still be seen today in the present Cemetery.

The imposing structure of St. Mark's Church of Ireland has been a focal point in Portadown since 1826 shortly after the parish had been created out of the Drumcree parish on the west of the Bann. The church was built on land, which previously housed the town stocks and gibbet – the latter of which was last used for a hanging in 1809! The church, which is built in blackstone with sandstone dressings, has been extended on a number of occasions over the years.

In Lurgan it is the Church of Christ The Redeemer, Church of Ireland, which is the dominant feature of the town centre. The building was originally erected in 1725 with a number of later enlargements. The steeple is made from the stones of the old church in Shankill graveyard some

Marjorie McCall's headstone, Shankill Cemetery, Lurgan

distance away, the previous wooden steeple having been blown down in 'The Big Wind of 1839.'

Shankill (from the Gaelic meaning Old Church) Burial Ground has a number of claims to fame – one being that it is the site of the Brownlow Memorial erected in 1737 as the mausoleum of the Brownlow family – the other being that it was what was thought to have been the 'final' resting place of Marjorie McCall. She had been buried but when a keen grave robber tried to steal a ring from her finger shortly after the funeral she was revived and returned to her astonished family in her shroud. The woman whose grave is marked with the legend 'Lived Once Buried Twice' finally died in 1711 – at least it is hoped she did!

St. Peter's Roman Catholic Church was also constructed in stages, between 1867 and 1927. Its spire dominates the

St. Mark's Church of Ireland, Portadown

Lurgan skyline being the tallest structure in the town. The site for the church was granted rent free in perpetuity by Lord Lurgan.

Presbyterian, Methodist, Baptist and churches of many other denominations abound throughout the Borough. While Methodists were influential in the establishment of Portadown's later commercial life it was undoubtedly the Quakers who played a major role in the prosperity of Lurgan with their influence in the linen industry. The land on which the Quaker Meeting House is sited was donated by Robert Hoope who arrived in Lurgan in 1664 and by 1700 had, through trading in linen, become its wealthiest citizen. As well as the Quaker graveyard in Lurgan, another exists at Lynastown which is reputed to be the oldest in Ireland. It is thought likely that the first Quaker Meeting took place in Lurgan in 1654 with the first burial taking place at Lynastown in 1658. The final burial took place in 1967 and the site has now been taken over by Craigavon Borough Council as a 'closed graveyard'.

1.

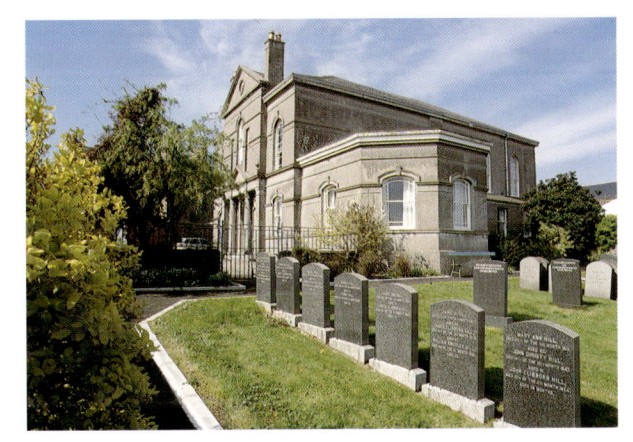

3.

1. Church of Christ The Redeemer, Church of Ireland, Lurgan
2. St. Peter's Parish Church, Roman Catholic Church, Lurgan
3. Quaker Graveyard, Lurgan
4. Holy Trinity Church of Ireland, Waringstown

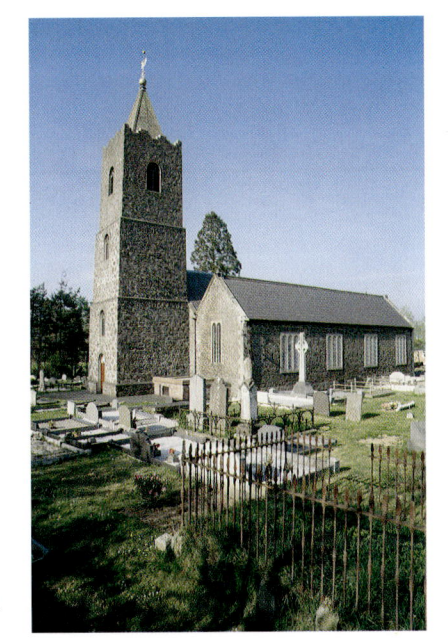

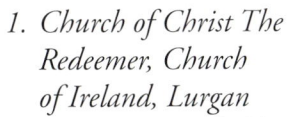

2.

4.

Urban and Civic Life

While the origins and early development of the area have been examined in an earlier section of the book there is much more to be said of recent developments and the civic aspect of the Borough.

The growth of Portadown is indicative of the general increase in population of the area over the centuries. Portadown consisted of only three small houses in the reign of Charles I (1619); 155 houses and 767 inhabitants in 1814 wheras today there is a population in excess of 24,000 in the town.

Due to the central position of Craigavon and the traditional commercial bases of the market towns, the area has witnessed quite a phenomenal development. The proximity of excellent communications by road and rail together with the educational, recreational, not to mention medical facilities provide the area with an excellent basis from which to compete with any other in the Province.

While multi-nationals have been attracted to the towns, the fact that there is still a good number of family-owned businesses give the towns that touch of charm and character which attracts the shopper. Both towns have wide and open main streets which creates a conducive atmosphere for shopping.

The architectural heritage of the buildings in the two main towns adds to their distinctive style and character. Portadown Town Hall is an attractive Victorian building now used as a meeting place for different groups as well as drama productions. Erected in 1890, the building was once home to the Portadown Borough Council before the amalgamation with Lurgan and the move to the Civic Centre in the central area.

Likewise Lurgan Town Hall, a listed Victorian building built in 1868, is now used for community and theatrical purposes, where once it housed the Lurgan Borough Council.

The Old Court House in William Street dates back to 1874 but was no longer required following the completion of a new Court House in central Craigavon. The building is now a Public House, bringing a whole new meaning to the expression – 'being called to the Bar'!

Brownlow is the central sector of Craigavon and was developed as a result of the decision in 1963 to create Craigavon as Northern Ireland's first New Town. Brownlow has developed,

Portadown Market

primarily as a dormitory area, on a modular system with neighbourhood centres to service the shopping and community needs of each of the housing areas.

Larger shopping centres together with various Central and Local Government offices, including the Civic Centre, are also located within the central area.

The Civic Centre, in addition to being the administrative centre of Craigavon Borough Council, performs a civic function as well, providing as it does a magnificent auditorium for concerts or shows; a banqueting suite and major conference facilities.

Craigavon can offer fine food and hospitality ranging from a restaurant in one of the oldest buildings in the Borough, The Grange in Waringstown, to the most modern hotel – the rebuilt Seagoe Hotel, Portadown.

Church Wall, Waringstown

1. Craigavon Civic Centre
2. Former Courthouse, Lurgan
3. The Grange, Waringstown
4. Seagoe Hotel, Portadown
5. Lurgan Town Hall
6. Street Scene, Lurgan
7. Portadown Town Hall
8. Portadown Markets Building
9. Market St. Portadown

Countryside

The Bannfoot

One of the aims of the 'New Town' planners was that all citizens should be within a mile of the countryside. There are plenty of places and opportunities in Craigavon to get away from it all. From the tranquility of the Riverside Walkway and Moneypenny's Lockhouse to the south of the Borough to Coney Island in the west, from the villages in the east to the shores of Lough Neagh in the north – and many points in between!

Lying just a half a mile off shore from Maghery is Coney Island in Lough Neagh. Archaeological digs indicate habitation dating back to pre-historic times as well as others in the 13th and 16th Centuries with old flints and arrowheads having been found. Formerly known as Innisdabhall and Sydney's Island, Coney Island was once linked to the mainland by a causeway called St. Patrick's Way. There is a stone on the island which tradition has it was once used by St. Patrick as a resting place. It is widely regarded as being the western outpost for the Normans during their occupation of Ireland. The Anglo-Norman motte was built as a stronghold in the 13th Century and the

Rare Breeds at Tannaghmore Gardens

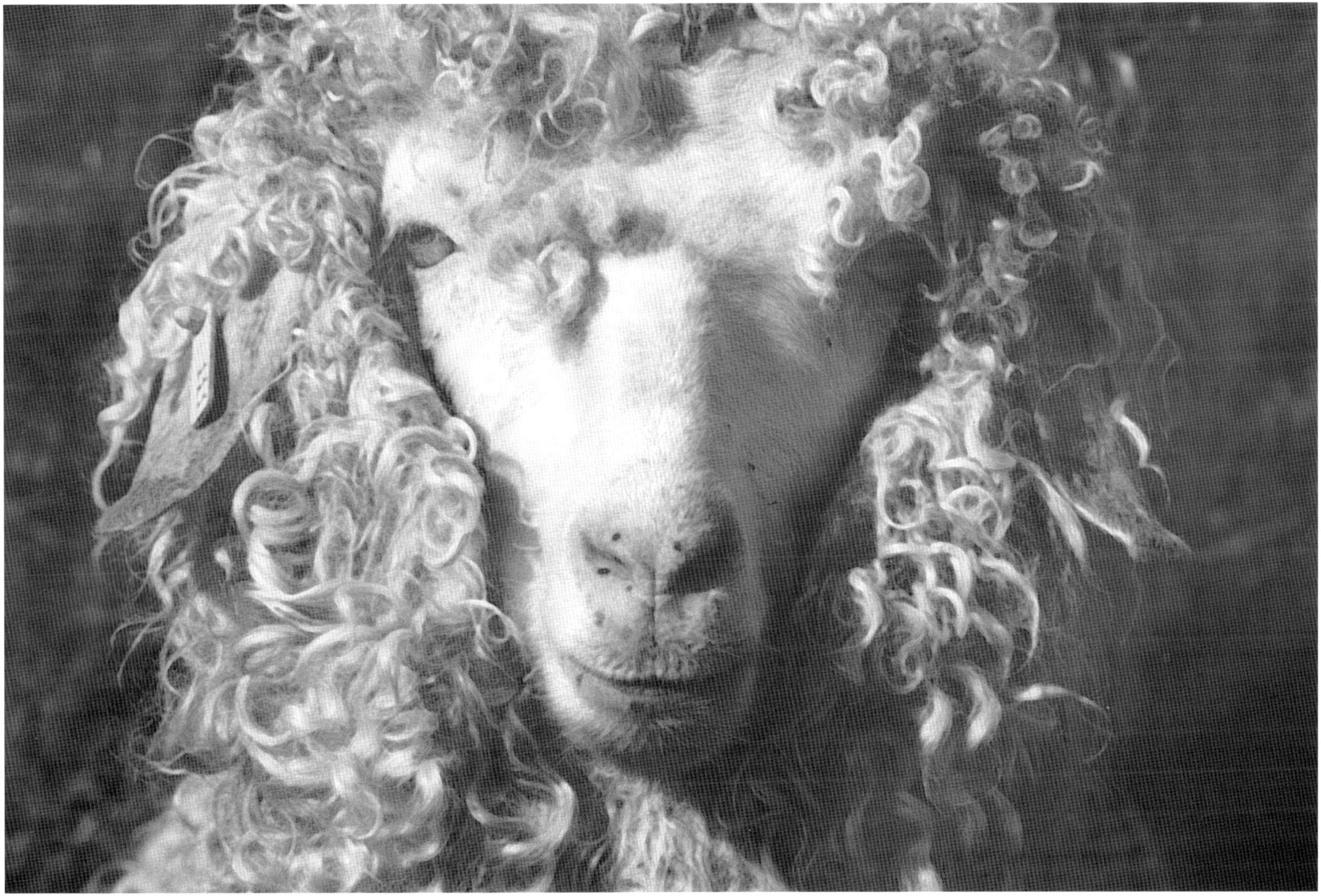

Newry to Portadown Canal

island was used as a penal colony in the 16th and 17th Centuries, with condemned men being beheaded on the mound. Then there is O'Neill's Tower that the clan used as a look out post against anyone who would seek to steal their valuables. Latterly Lord Charlemont built the Victorian cottage in 1885 as a summer retreat and he loved the place so much that it is his final resting place. The island was placed into the hands of the National Trust but it was not until the early 1980s when Craigavon Borough Council agreed to manage the property that its condition was restored and a full-time warden appointed. The island covers over seven acres and the conservation aspects of the island are promoted by the Council.

With a major part of Craigavon being in Co. Armagh, the 'Orchard County of Ireland' it is not surprising that one of the main fruit crops is the apple. Apple Blossom tours are organised each year around the main orchards to show off the beautiful pink blossoms.

Swans, Lurgan Park

Leisure and Recreation

Lough Neagh Discovery Centre

Among the many assets, of which Craigavon can boast, is its range and quality of sport and leisure facilities. The Council is a leading provider of a wide range of high standard facilities for both indoor and outdoor activities in the Province. In addition to the natural assets of Lough Neagh and the River Bann, the area has a lot to offer.

The Borough is unique in providing a high quality golf course and Northern Ireland's premier artificial ski-slope, on the same site at Silverwood, Lurgan. As well as the three golf courses on site at Silverwood there are three others throughout the Borough offering the enthusiast plenty of challenge.

With so much water throughout the Borough it is perhaps not surprising that watersports are a major specialism. The Centre of Excellence at the Watersports Centre is renowned throughout the Province offering instruction in water skiing, jet skiing, canoeing and windsurfing. Kinnego Marina on Lough Neagh provides 90 fully sheltered berths and on-shore facilities for boat owners from all over Northern Ireland with sailing and power boat instruction being available.

Each of the main centres of population is served by its own local leisure complex – Waves in Lurgan has a swimming pool with wave machine while Cascades in Portadown offers the opportunity of a 'splashing' time with its flumes and diving area. Both centres have fitness suites as does the Craigavon Leisure Centre in Brownlow which offers swimming pool and sports halls as well.

Soccer also features highly in the

Award for Best Project, is a fine example of the way in which traditional craft is being carried on. The visitor will be able to view the potters at work creating the hand thrown and decorated stoneware. It is located in Bloomvale House, a very apt setting as the house was built in 1785 by the Gaskin family. The Gaskins were French Huguenots who, having fled France travelled to Ireland bringing with them their traditional skills and knowledge of the Linen Industry. Craigavon is part of the Linen Homelands route which visitors can follow to learn more of the industry which is now in decline due to less expensive synthetic materials coming to the fore. The firm of Ewart Liddell continues to manufacture linen products for major airlines and hotels at their factory premises which started in Donaghcloney in 1866. Though the looms are obviously modern the traditional skill and attention to quality are still paramount. Among the Company's famous products were linens for the ill-fated SS Titanic.

Basket Weaver

Arts and Crafts

The Borough has a lively Arts scene which includes the long running Portadown Music, Drama and Dance Festival Competitions. Amateur dramatics is very popular with frequent performances being given in the two Town Halls. The Markets Building is soon to be redeveloped through an initiative of Portadown 2000 working in partnership with the Council and Kaleidoscope to provide a verbal and visual Arts Centre as part of an overall scheme. The Peacock Gallery and Arts Centre is situated at Pinebank House and caters for exhibitions of both local and international visual arts.

The people of Craigavon are very industrious and as well as the advanced computer technology which is abundant in the Borough there is a desire to protect and uphold the traditional methods of doing things. A good number of thatched cottages remain, indeed some modern houses are now reverting to this traditional, if expensive, method of roofing.

Among the crafts that are present are basket weaving, copper working, boat building, iron craft, traditional jewellery and of course pottery. Ballydougan Pottery, recently the winner of the British Airways Tourism

Boat Builder

Ballydougan Pottery

Linen worker at Ewart Liddell

1. 18th Century Hugeonot
   Farmhouse (now Ballydougan Pottery)
2. & 3. Traditional Windows
4. Moneypenny's Lockhouse on
   Newry/Portadown Canal
5. Tannaghmore Gardens
6. The Old Mill, Donaghcloney

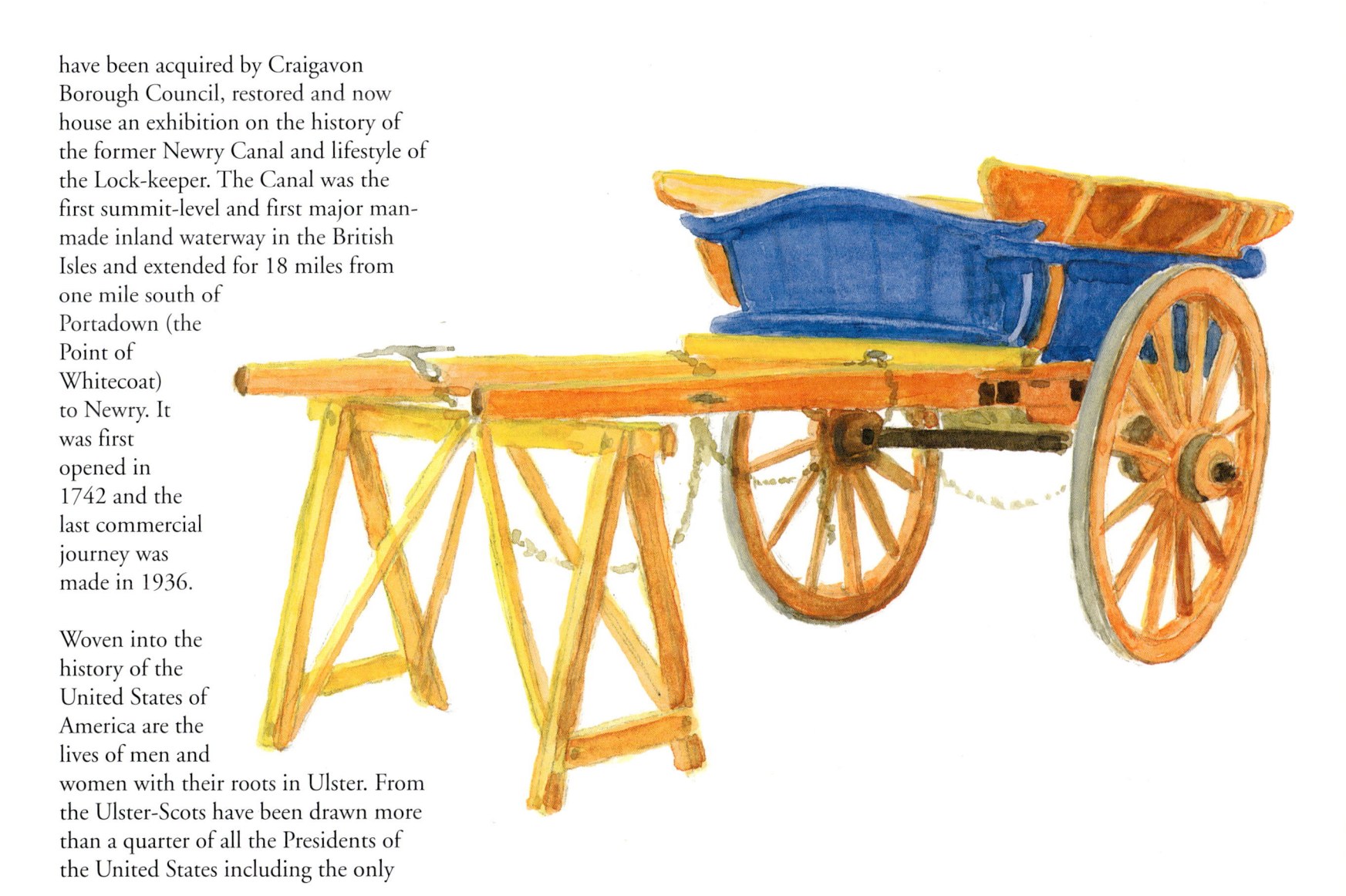

have been acquired by Craigavon Borough Council, restored and now house an exhibition on the history of the former Newry Canal and lifestyle of the Lock-keeper. The Canal was the first summit-level and first major man-made inland waterway in the British Isles and extended for 18 miles from one mile south of Portadown (the Point of Whitecoat) to Newry. It was first opened in 1742 and the last commercial journey was made in 1936.

Woven into the history of the United States of America are the lives of men and women with their roots in Ulster. From the Ulster-Scots have been drawn more than a quarter of all the Presidents of the United States including the only

Gilbert's Mill, Aghagallon

Gilbert's Mill at Aghagallon is currently being restored by the family as a working mill and museum with traditional farm machinery and walks along the millstream.

three first generation Americans to achieve the office. The Birches boasts of the ancestral home of General 'Stonewall' Jackson, perhaps the best known of the 'fighting Ulster-Scots'. His grandfather, John Jackson, went to America in around 1748 having left his Birches home. James Logan was born in 1674 in Lurgan, where a plaque records that he moved to the United States and became President of the Council of Pennsylvania.

The Council's Museum Services house a library of local history books as well as an antiquarian collection of Quaker books. The museum has an exhibition outlet in the Barn Museum in Tannaghmore Gardens.

Coney Island

1.

Times Past

As new modes of transport and manufacture came into being, so the old declined. This can be seen in the disused railway tracks, canals and mills dotted throughout the Borough. However there has been a renaissance of interest in the traditional with plans for the protection and restoration of the things which once played such a significant role in the life and commerce of the Borough.

When one thinks of Harland & Wolfe shipbuilders the Titanic comes to mind but what of the smallest vessel ever made by that Company? The Bannfoot Ferry consisted of a floating platform at the point where the River Bann entered Lough Neagh and the ferryman used to haul on a rope to take cars and passengers across the river. The fare of 10 shillings (50p) was paid to avoid a 16-mile detour via Portadown. The ferry service, which was called upon at all hours of the day and night, was ended when the ferryman grew unable to cope with the work. All attempts to have a replacement ferry or bridge to save the local people of the Birches/Maghery/Bannfoot area the inconvenience of taking the long road, have so far been unsuccessful. However with the success of finding the Titanic – who knows! The ferry had a much better safety record after all!

Moneypenny's Lockhouse, which dates back to the beginning of the 19th Century, and the lighterman's bothy (cottage) are located adjacent to the Portadown Riverside Parkway. They

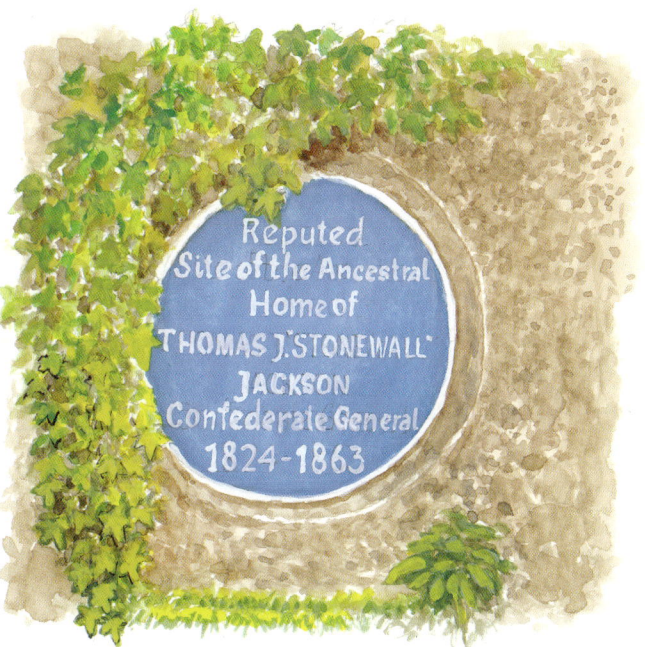

Stonewall Jackson's Ancestral Home, Birches

Waringstown House

Gatepost at Waringstown House

notably as the headquarters for various army regiments during the First and Second World Wars. General George Patton used the property as a military HQ in September 1943. It is reputed that General Dwight D. Eisenhower, later President of the USA, stayed overnight in the bedroom formerly belonging to Lord Lurgan. Who knows – it may have been when there that he dreamt up the concept of Sister City International!

Also in the grounds is a stone obelisk which is associated with the famous greyhound – Master McGrath, named after the stable boy who trained the 'runt' of the litter and later bought back by Lord Lurgan – which won the Waterloo Cup on three occasions. The greyhound was paraded before Queen Victoria on one occasion due to its prowess on the track and its exploits are recorded in a ballad.

Waringstown, which is one of Ireland's most charming and picturesque villages, was founded in 1667 by William Waring who in the same year built his residence in the Jacobean style. The princely sum of £535 opened the door

Doorway, Fairview House, Tannaghmore

Entrance Door Brownlow House, Lurgan

to the house at the time of its completion! The property, which is still in its original form, was one of the first unfortified country houses to be erected in the land. The spacious gardens are full of rare specimens of trees, flora and fauna. It is believed that it was Mr Waring's attitude towards and treatment of his tenants which allowed the property to survive in what were very troubled times in Ireland's history. William Waring came from a tanning and weaving family and he, with his son, were instrumental in introducing damask weaving throughout Ireland at the end of the 17th Century.

Brownlow House, Lurgan

Stately Homes

Waringstown House

Among the many examples of fine architectural structures remaining in the Borough, Brownlow House (or Castle as it is often referred to) and Waringstown House must rank among the jewels in the crown.

During the Plantation of Ulster under James I, John Brownlow was granted an area of 1,500 acres in 1610 at a rent of £8 to hold in perpetuity. John's son William was also granted 1,000 acres in 1610 and it was he who, following the death of his father, was regranted the lands by Charles II in 1629. In later generations when there were no male heirs Lettice Brownlow became heiress to the Lurgan property. Her eldest son assumed the name of Brownlow. A descendent, Charles, built what was known as Lurgan House in 1833. It later became Brownlow House when Charles was made a peer in 1839. The building itself was built in the Elizabethan style using freestone imported from Scotland.

The house also contains parts of an older house dating back to the 17th Century. The 'modern' house was deigned by the renowned Scottish architect, William Henry Playfair, whose many fine Greek Revival buildings in Scotland helped earn Edinburgh the nickname 'Athens of the North'.

The house is reputed to have around 365 rooms and each of the tall spiral chimney pots is considered to be unique. The house was set in an estate of around 259 acres. The lake and much of the Lurgan property owned by the Brownlow family was sold to Lurgan Borough Council in 1893 for the princely sum of £2,000. The house has had a number of uses over the years,

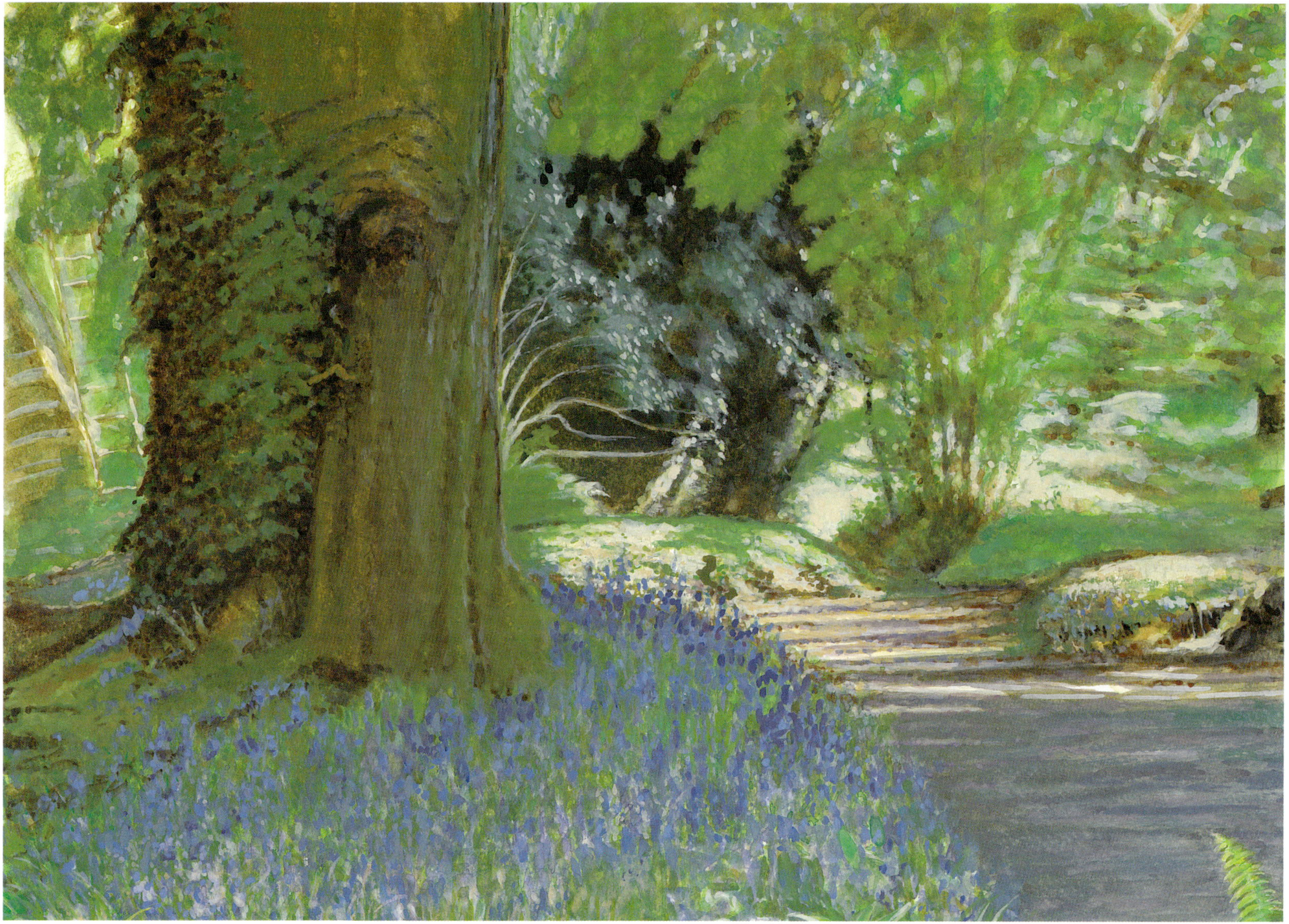

Portadown Riverside Walkway along the River Bann

around the City Lakes, adjacent to the Civic Centre. The lakes were also man-made and are now enjoyed by many who engage in watersports. The Central Park stretches from the Water Sports Centre with over 5 km of walkways. One of the walkways connects with Tannaghmore Gardens and Animal Farm. The linear parklands of the Brownlow area in Central Craigavon provide pleasant landscaped areas in the housing areas developed in the early 1970s.

The ongoing development of the Portadown Riverside Parkway has allowed people to once again enjoy the River as in yesteryear. It forms part of the Ulster Way running from the Boat Club to the Borough boundary at Moneypenny's Lockhouse on the Newry Canal.

Throughout the 1800s the town was one of the busiest inland ports in Ireland – thanks to a system of canals linking with the river it was possible to sail from Portadown to England and Scotland via Lough Neagh and the Lagan Navigation. Both sides of the river would have been busy with the Town Quay on one side and the Foundry slipway on the other where small boats would be launched a few yards away from the pleasure craft at the then Boat House site. The decline in use of the waterways came with the increased use of the railway and for a long time the town turned its back on the river but this is now changing with a revival in the fortunes of Irish Canals, there is a lot of interest in the possibility of re-opening the Newry to Portadown canal. The People's Park in Portadown was gifted by the Duke of Manchester who owned much of the land on which the town was built.

Bluebells on Coney Island, Maghery

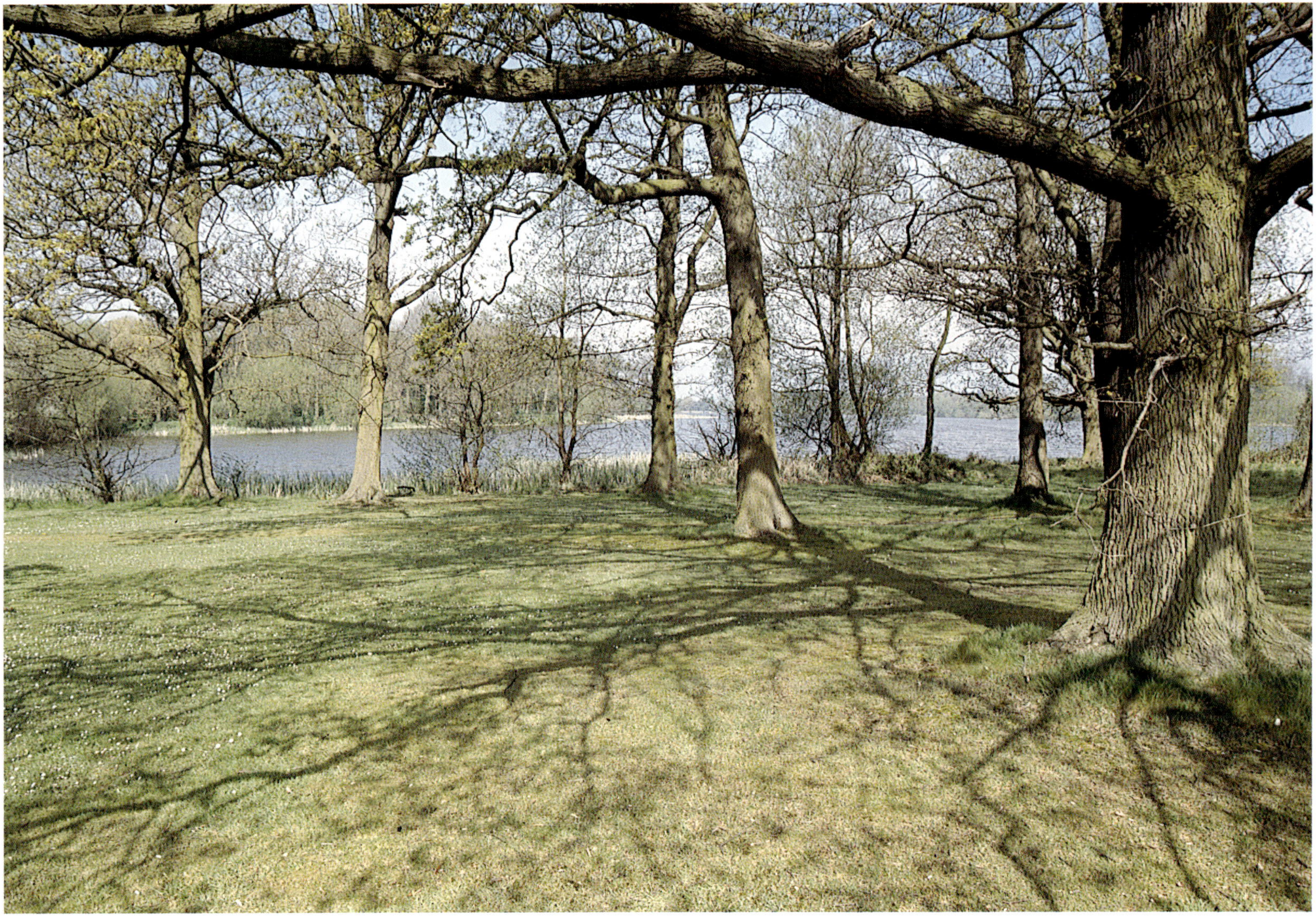

Parklands

Cherry Blossom in Lurgan Park

Parks and landscaping are a very obvious feature of Craigavon with a total of nine town parks, four linear parks and three rural parks offering a total in excess of 1,000 acres of park open space throughout the Borough. These parklands not only provide a convenient location for sport and leisure activities but also serve to create a pleasant and green environment in the busyness of town life. An emphasis on neatness has been traditional over the years. The famous English writer, William Makepeace Thackery on a visit to Ireland in the 19th Century, described how he enjoyed walking through Portadown during a break in his journey. He found it to be a very neat and well laid out town – 'a pleasant and attractive place'.

Lurgan, likewise, boasts a splendid park, formerly the Demesne of the Brownlow family with a man-made lake dug during the Famine as a means of creating jobs for the locals. Though greatly altered for recreational purposes the grounds still form one of the finest town parks in Ulster. Lord Lurgan Memorial Park was granted in perpetuity to the Council by the Brownlows as a place for leisure and recreation.

Maghery Country Park is situated on the shores of Lough Neagh, covering an area of 30 acres it offers some of the best views of the Lough, Coney Island, and the mountains of Counties Antrim, Down and Tyrone.

Another major park is the Central Park

Lurgan Park Lak

The supporters are a Unicorn inspired by the Armorial Bearings of Lurgan, bearing flax to represent the historic linen industry of the town and an Antelope from the Armorial Bearings of Portadown in reference to the Dukes of Manchester who owned the land. The Antelope bears the Seagoe Bell, an ancient bell of that parish. Both stand on a rural grassy mound scattered with apples, the celebrated local fruit, and shamrock. The symbolic water represents the River Bann and Craigavon Lakes.

Lough Neagh

Mr. and Mrs. Hall travelling in Ireland in 1840 wrote: -

'There is no country in the world so safe or so pleasant for strangers, so that for every new visitor it receives, it will obtain a new friend. In driving to the magnificent Lough Neagh we passed through a singular district called the Munches (Montiaghs, meaning bogland). Let the reader imagine a tract of bog stretching far and away. At the termination of this outspread bog we came into sight of Lough Neagh and, standing upon its banks, we saw, as it were, a sea encompassed by land.'

With shores in five of the six counties of Northern Ireland, Lough Neagh is the largest freshwater lake in the British Isles. The Lough abounds in legends relating to its origins. One of the best known is that of Ireland's legendary giant, Finn McCool, he of the Giant's Causeway fame, who is said to have created the Lough when one day he scooped up a portion of the land to toss it at a Scottish rival. He missed and the earth landed in the Irish Sea thereby creating the Isle of Man. The space left behind became filled with water and became Lough Neagh! A more scientific theory would suggest that the Lough came about as a result of a volcanic eruption many years ago which produced a large expanse of water 17 miles long by 11 miles wide.

Today Lough Neagh is internationally recognised for its nature conservation value especially its large population of wildfowl. The Lough is also an important source of water supply and is the largest inland fishery in Europe. Its eel fishery interests are very lucrative as the eels have proved a very popular delicacy in the top European hotels.

Industry

Craigavon, with 40% of the Northern Ireland industrial base outside Belfast, supports a mixed economy with particular emphasis on export focused manufacturing in the following sectors: – food processing, plastics, pharmaceuticals, light engineering/metal fabrication; and carpet manufacturing/textiles. The medical products, electronic and service sectors are very strong in the area. Agriculture is also significant with dairy, beef and sheep farming representing over 50% of this sector.

remains of one of the old Granges of the Abbey of St. Peter and St. Paul at Armagh, while nearby stands the impressive ruins of O'Connor's Castle on Derrawarragh Island with Coney Island a short distance across the Lough.

Magheralin has several fine examples of planters' houses such as Drumcro and Blacklion. The local parish church is one of the best in Ulster in which to see the works of Irish artists in stained glass with windows depicting six saints of the North. The tower and nave of the original church, the foundations of which date back to medieval times, can still be seen in the village as well.

Waringstown (of which more will be said of its founder later in the book) was noted for many years on account of its handloom damask weaving. The village is also famous for its cricket and the cricket ground known as 'The Lawn' which ranks as one of the most sylvan settings that the game has in the whole of Ireland.

Waringstown has received national and international recognition for its architecture and even more often for its landscaping and floral displays with nominations to the 'Entente Floral' competition. It has also received a number of 'Best Kept Small Town' awards.

Armorial Bearings

Craigavon Borough Council came into being in October 1973 following the reorganisation of Local Government. The Armorial Bearings were designed to retain some of the historical elements pertaining to the two main towns of Lurgan and Portadown while at the same time the motto 'Together We Progress' refers to their amalgamation in the new urban development concept of Craigavon.

On the crown stands Master McGrath, the famous greyhound owned by the Brownlow family of Lurgan and winner of the Waterloo Cup. He holds a wheel tapper as a reference to the importance of Portadown as a railway junction. The shield is indented to depict the joining of the two town Boroughs and surrounding the Red Hand of Ulster are four woven gold strands representing linen manufacture. Roundels symbolising coins and cogs in the centre of each roundel depict other industry. The Red Hand of Ulster is the well known insignia of the O'Neills who were at one time the principal clan in Ulster and whose main territory lay on both sides of the Upper Bann and around Lough Neagh. Legend goes that a rival was pursuing the O'Neill, of many centuries ago, who arrived by boat from Scotland. He wanted to lay claim to the land and in order to be the first to 'lay hand' to the claim, cut off one hand and threw it to the shore.

Armstrong and Castleisland. Hemstitching factories making up linen products appeared from 1872 onwards including the famous names of Hamilton Robb, Spence Bryson, Luttons, Dawsons and Cowdys.

However the real impetus for the town's development with regard to transportation was, undoubtedly, the building of the railway line from Belfast. This reached the town by 1842 and by the 1870s, Portadown was one of the busiest rail junctions in Ireland with links to Armagh, Belfast, Dublin and Londonderry earning it the nickname of 'Hub of the North'.

On the international scene, one of Portadown's main claims to fame was rose growing and in particular the roses of Sam McGready & Son. For over a century these roses were sent to the furthermost parts of the globe until in 1976 the company moved to one of those far-off points – New Zealand.

Lurgan was first named in a grant dated 1629 to William Brownlow, of whom more will be said later in the book, giving him permission to hold a weekly market and two annual fairs. The area had originally been called 'Lurga bhaile mhac Cann' meaning 'the long ridge townland of the McCanns'. The reference to the long ridge is clearly evident today with the lands to the rear of the main street sloping quite steeply down on either side.

Lurgan became established as a market town in the 17th Century following the arrival of the Brownlow family but it was the linen industry which gave the impetus to the town's economic development and expansion over the ensuing centuries. As long ago as 1682 it was said that in and around Lurgan there was carried on the 'greatest linen manufacture in Ireland'.

The essential character of the town has remained as it would have been over a century ago. The alleyways and laneways off the town centre reveal the gardens, tenements, factories and indeed farm buildings which were once typical of the town.

The Union Workhouse, which housed those less fortunate citizens of yesteryear, still stands and has been incorporated into the Lurgan Hospital building. The last inhabitant of the workhouse, at the time of its closure remained to serve as a maid to the Matron of the 'new' hospital.

Craigavon has many villages and small settlements scattered throughout the Borough including Aghagallon, Birches, Bleary, Charlestown/Bannfoot, Derrytrasna, Dollingstown, Donaghcloney, Magheralin, Maghery and Waringstown.

All are unique in their own right with individual characteristics reflecting their origins and development. Of special note are: -

Maghery, situated at the southwest corner of Lough Neagh, is well off the beaten track but popular with boating enthusiasts and caravaners. In the graveyard at St Mary's Church are the

Bann that flows from the south east to the north west into Lough Neagh.

The area is surrounded by undulating hills to the east, south and west. Much of the area is also given over to mixed agriculture including cattle, cereals and fruit growing.

A major feature of Craigavon is its transport communications network. The Borough is transversed by the M1 motorway linking Belfast with Dungannon and is also on the main cross-border corridor leading through Armagh to Monaghan. Craigavon sits astride the main Belfast – Dublin railway line with commuter stations at both Lurgan and Portadown. It also enjoys easy access to the ports and airports.

The Borough has an estimated population of 79,000 with the main towns of Lurgan and Portadown accounting for 46,000 between them, Brownlow 8,000, main villages 13,000 and the rural areas 12,000.

Borough Towns and Villages

Portadown which derives its name from the Gaelic 'Port-ne-Dun' (Port of the Fortress) associated with the powerful local McCann family who were among the area's earliest settlers.

The town's modern history commenced in the 17th Century with the Ulster Plantation but there is evidence that people lived in the vicinity as long ago as 2000BC. A church at Mahon was associated with St. Patrick and indeed there still exists a well which is named after the saint at the locality. The town featured strongly in the 1641 Rebellion against the Plantation when a number of settlers were drowned in the River Bann. The River Bann (the White River) has always played a major role in the life of the town and its environs. The Obins family was very keen to develop the area and as early as 1703 Anthony Obins was involved in the first survey for a canal to link the River Bann with Newry and the Irish Sea. The town's first stone bridge was erected in 1763/4 but in 1765 due to floods, three of its seven arches collapsed. Several more bridges followed before the present granite structure was completed. It is rumoured that the current bridge was actually built on dry land, following which a new bed was dug to bring the river under it!

Bridges continue to play an important role in modern Portadown as to enter the town one has to either cross a bridge or travel under one!

Linen manufacture was one of the town's earliest industries and in 1762 Michael Obins petitioned the Irish House of Commons to set up a linen market. This was followed in 1780 with the creation of a grain market. Both markets benefited from the cheap supply of water transport via the River and the Newry Canal, which also played a significant role in the town's increasing importance as a manufacturing and trading centre. There were many weaving firms, including Achesons, Watson

Craigavon

Situated on the southern shore of Lough Neagh the Borough of Craigavon covers an area of approximately 100 square miles. It borders Lisburn to the north, Armagh to the south and has within its border parts of Counties Armagh, Antrim and Down.

Occupying this significant and central location in Northern Ireland, Craigavon is based on the two historic market towns of Lurgan and Portadown. The third major centre of population is the area of Brownlow, situated between the two towns. There are also a number of villages and hamlets set in some of the Province's most pleasant countryside, sheltered within the valleys of the River Bann and River Lagan.

History & Geography

While there is some evidence of early pre-Christian settlements in the region, it was the establishment of the ancient city of Armagh as Ireland's ecclesiastical capital which served in consolidating many small hamlets into villages and towns over the centuries.

By the mid 17th Century the area had become an important and relatively wealthy agricultural region. However, it is to the industrial revolution in the late 18th Century and the development of the linen industry that the present day towns of Lurgan and Portadown owe their economic prosperity.

The development of canal navigation completed in 1741 between Newry, at Carlingford Lough – with its access to the Irish Sea, and Lough Neagh, and the later development of Ireland's railway network, served to open up the area as a key-manufacturing centre.

The potential of the area as a modern industrial centre with scope for development was one of the key reasons for establishing Craigavon New Town following a proposal by Professor Sir Robert Matthew in1963. The New Town was to provide a large industrial, commercial and residential base to relieve the urban pressure on Belfast and to contribute to the rejuvenation of the south and west of the Province.

Craigavon's main geographic characteristics are an extensive shoreline to the north, the level landscape and the extensive natural drainage network centring on the slow moving River

The Artist

with the Council, Lewis has a number of roles including that of Sister City International Liaison Officer.

Lewis was instrumental in establishing the link with LaGrange in 1993 and has visited Craigavon's Sister City on numerous occasions since then, planning projects and exchanges to further develop the relationship and bring benefits to as wide a spectrum of people as possible.

He has a keen interest in the development of the Borough having been involved in Lurgan Forward and Portadown 2000 Town Development Companies since their inception, serving each initially as Company Secretary and subsequently as a Director.

Born in the former Yugoslavia, Alex B. Kalinin was educated in England before migrating to Canada and thence to Beaufort S.C. He moved to Georgia in 1981 where he maintains his studio in a lovely century old Victorian home with his wife Anne at the Anne Tutt Gallery near Callaway Gardens.

Alex's masterful handling of light and color and his romantic approach to his subjects have led him to be chosen for many corporate and private collections.

A growing collection of fine art collector prints including vibrant landscapes of Callaway Gardens, North Georgia Mountain scenes, Peach orchards etc, show how warmly Alex has embraced Georgia and the South. Their tremendous variety provides many subjects for his paintings although he also draws ideas from further afield; "I've discovered inspiration as near as our own back garden and constantly at Georgia's beautiful Callaway Gardens and as far as Pateley Bridge, Yorkshire or the fabulous Hawaiian and California golf courses. One needs an eternity and then some to paint his inspirations!"

The Photographer

J ohn D. Lawrence, Callaway Professor of Art, is Chairman of the Humanities and Fine Arts Division of LaGrange College and Director of the Lamar Dodd Art Center. Mr Lawrence studied at Millsapps College in Jackson, Mississippi, and received a Bachelor of Fine Arts degree from Tulane University. He joined the faculty at LaGrange College in 1970. Since that time he has been active in the cultural life of LaGrange as well as Georgia and the Southeast area in general. He is a regular speaker at civic clubs, colleges and art related meetings and has served as juror of many exhibitions throughout the Southeast. As the Director of the Lamar Dodd Art Center, he has established one of the country's largest college museum collections of 20th century photography. Mr Lawrence's photographic expertise has seen him participate in several exhibitions in the United States and Europe and his work has featured in many publications.

The Author

B orn in Portadown, Lewis Porter joined Craigavon Borough Council in 1983 after graduating with a Joint Honours degree from Queen's University Belfast.

As a Principal Administrative Officer

Preamble

This publication seeks to celebrate and highlight the significance of the relationship which has been developing between Craigavon, Northern Ireland and LaGrange, Georgia, USA, since contact was first made in 1993. The formalisation of the linkage in 1996 through Sister City International became the catalyst for a programme of civic, cultural, sport, business and education exchanges.

The photographs and paintings reflect the perceptions of the photographers and artists, from the communities involved, following visits to their respective Sister Cities. It is by no means an exhaustive authority on the history of the areas involved nor does it claim to have captured all the facets of life that exists in them. It is hoped, however, that through the images and text, the appetite of the reader will be whet to the extent that they will wish to visit their Sister City. If it further inspires them to get involved with the work of the LaGrange International Friendship Exchange (LIFE) Committee or the Craigavon Sister City International Committee to extend the benefits of the relationship to a greater number of citizens then so much the better.

Acknowledgements

I would wish to thank all those who contributed their time and services in making this publication possible. To Craigavon Borough Council for its sponsorship; the Sister City International Committee for supporting the idea when I first suggested it, especially the Chairman, Councillor Kenneth Twyble for his encouragement and Cathy McShane for help in selecting the artist and photographer, ideas on the format and helping to keep things sane!; Rosaleen McMullan, the Council's Arts Development Officer; Sharon Magee for all her very able assistance; Margaret Ross for co-ordinating and cajoling – with 'hugs' – on the LaGrange end; Myrtle Porter for showing me the importance of offering hospitality; and Sadie, Zara and Adam for their patient endurance, especially as the deadline for the text approached.

Thanks are also due to those whose properties we visited and who gave of their time to communicate their love for their heritage, skills and land.

Lewis Porter

First published by Cottage Publications,
Donaghadee, N. Ireland 1999.
Copyrights Reserved.
© Craigavon SCI Committee / LIFE
All rights reserved.
No part of this book may be reproduced or
stored on any media without the express
written permission of the publishers.
Design & origination in Northern Ireland.
Printed & bound in Singapore.

ISBN 1 900935 14 7

Craigavon LaGrange

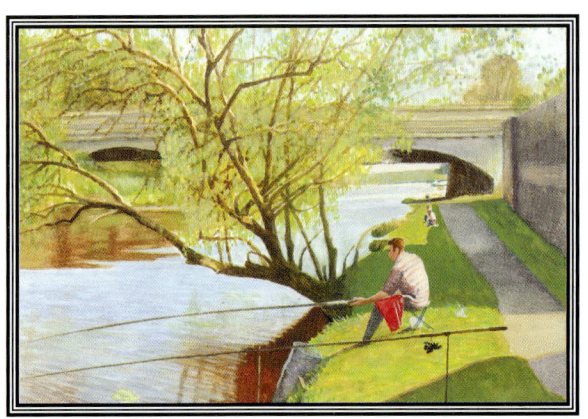

Craigavon

Alex Kalinin · John Lawrence · Lewis Porter

Cottage Publications